G000065864

Symbolism and Folk Imagery IN EARLY EGYPTIAN POLITICAL CARICATURES

Utah Series
IN MIDDLE E

Byron D. Cannon

Foreword by Samir Toubassy

Symbolism and Folk Imagery
IN EARLY EGYPTIAN
POLITICAL CARICATURES

The Wafd Election Campaign, 1920–1923

The University of Utah Press | Salt Lake City

*Full-color publication of this book is made possible in part
by the generous financial support of Samir Toubassy.*

Copyright © 2019 by The University of Utah Press. All rights reserved.

 The Defiance House Man colophon is a registered trademark of The University of
Utah Press. It is based on a four-foot-tall Ancient Puebloan pictograph (late PIII)
near Glen Canyon, Utah.

Library of Congress Cataloging-in-Publication Data

Names: Cannon, Byron, 1940– author.
Title: Symbolism and folk imagery in early Egyptian political caricatures : the Wafd election
    campaign, 1920–1923 / by Byron D. Cannon.
Description: Salt Lake City : The University of Utah Press, [2019] | Series: Utah series in Middle
    East studies | Includes bibliographical references and index.
Identifiers: LCCN 2018052928 (print) | LCCN 2018055006 (ebook) | ISBN 9781607817000 () |
    ISBN 9781607816997 (cloth : alk. paper)
Subjects: LCSH: Political campaigns—Egypt—Caricatures and cartoons—History–20th
    century. | Egypt—Politics and government—Caricatures and cartoons—20th cen-
    tury. | Egypt—Politics and government—Humor—20th century. | Egypt—Politics and
    government—1919–1952.
Classification: LCC DT107.8 (ebook) | LCC DT107.8 .C325 2019 (print) |
    DDC 324.70962/09042—dc23
LC record available at https://lccn.loc.gov/2018052928

Errata and further information on this and other titles available online at UofUpress.com

Printed and bound in the United States of America.

CONTENTS

ILLUSTRATIONS

NOTE ON TRANSLITERATION

To simplify transliteration of widely recognized Arabic or Turkish proper nouns, personal or place names (e.g., Quran, Saad Zaghlul, Topkapi, etc.), standard roman alphabet spellings are used throughout. Titles of Arabic newspapers or books and more complex Arabic phrases that appear in the text are transliterated following the *International Journal of Middle East Studies* system. Again, however, for simplification the article *al-* before nouns will appear without distinction between "solar" (*Ḥurūf shamsiyya*) or "lunar" (*Ḥurūf qamariyya*) first letters. When Arabic or Turkish material is from a primary or secondary source quoted in this text, the original author's transliteration is carried over from the source quoted.

In 2011, Robert D. Newman, then dean of the College of Humanities, invited me to an impressive exhibition of Egyptian political posters sponsored by the Middle East Center at the University of Utah. The works on display included treasures of early-twentieth century Wafd Party political art that I thought needed to more widely seen. The exhibition occurred at a time of political upheaval, when the Arab Spring promised a radical shift toward freedom and progressive changes in Egypt and the rest of the Arab world.

To me, this seemed an opportune time to introduce a new generation to the political cari-catures created during the Saad Zagloul Wafd Party–era and show how a political party in 1920 adopted and worked toward the same principles that youth were still calling for in 2011. Senior people at Utah, as well as the presidents of the American University of Beirut and the American University in Cairo, agreed with me that the material needed to be published. But it was when I was introduced to Dr. Byron D. Cannon, emeritus professor of history at the University of Utah, that a project began to take shape, as he shared my interest in these posters.

I met several times with various people at the University of Utah Press and the J. Willard Marriott Library, including the Press's editor-in-chief, Dr. John Alley; Dr. Gregory Thompson, associate dean and head of Special Collections; Dr. Leonard Chiarelli, the library's Middle East Librarian; and Glenda Cotter, the Press's director. At these meetings I always shared my ideas and expressed my enthusiasm and support for the emerging book project, as I did in lunch meetings with Dr. Cannon in Park City. Before it was decided to focus on the historical aspects of the Wafd's political posters, it seemed possible that I might even contribute a chapter or two on the Wafd Party as it exists today.

I was occasionally briefed on progress during the several years it took Dr. Cannon to write, revise, and have his manuscript approved for publication. When it finally became obvious that the only way to really do justice to the political art found here was to publish it in full color, I was pleased to help make this possible. All published books at some point become collabo-rative efforts between the author, the publisher, and hands-on supporters, and I am pleased to have been part of the effort that created *Symbolism and Folk Imagery in Early Egyptian Political Caricatures: The Wafd Election Campaign, 1920–1923.*

Samir Toubassy
August 2019

It is rare when nearly forgotten primary source materials surface that may throw new light on historical subjects already studied widely by recognized scholars. Such finds are particularly important if they suggest links to other sources that can be exploited in ways that were not apparent earlier. In this case, the challenge involves reexamining peculiar circumstances surrounding the emergence of political caricature art in early twentieth-century Egypt and eventually the ways in which such popular art changed form and content by the century's end.

The story of this process of change begins with a rare collection of original lithographs from early twentieth-century Egypt held in the Special Collections Department of the J. Willard Marriott Library of the University of Utah. As the project took form, a number of very similar lithographs from the early twentieth century came to light in a collection belonging to a private individual in Cairo, Mrs. Lesley Lababidi, who generously offered access to her holdings. Most of these added materials were done by the same artists and printed by the same lithograph presses as those that led to the original J. Willard Marriott Library project. A few were duplicates, but many offered interesting variants that revisit themes contained in the University of Utah collection.[1] Correspondence with three descendants of the man who was perhaps the most prominent Egyptian artist doing lithographic printing in this period—one Abdel Hamid Zaki—enabled me to obtain valuable information concerning the provenance of items in both collections. I thank Dr. Nehal El Naggar, her mother, Malak El Badrawy, and her daughter Malak Fawzy for sharing elements of their family's heritage with me. Research into possible provenance for the original graphics was further compounded by the discovery of other nearly contemporary lithographs— definitely related, but representing different historically important subjects—in several major world libraries, including the British Museum, the Library of Congress, and the Hoover Institution at Stanford University. In addition, copies of original works from various websites offer still different perspectives when compared with the "rediscovered" Egyptian documents that launched this research.

This book focuses on graphic images connected with the early stages of nationalist politics spearheaded by the Egyptian Wafd ("Delegation") immediately after World War I.[2] One might suppose, therefore, that the discussion is intended for a restricted audience—one already familiar with the specific historical setting and interested in what these graphics can tell us about events occurring in that particular context. In part, that is true. But, as the project progressed, several things became apparent. First was the discovery that these original examples of early lithographs from Egypt represent only one, albeit a very important, part of a developing "trade" linking commercial artists and printers to a modest local consumer market in several regions of the late Ottoman Empire. Interests among local purchasers of such graphics probably ranged from a desire for simple household decorative illustrations to a more or less conscious desire to identify with nationalist political symbols just appearing in the region, and, more specifically with the emergence of the Wafd movement in Egypt at that time.

Even though the technical artistic level and mode of caricatural art in most of these lithographs is rather elementary, they merit recognition as part of a broader field of art history. Early turn-of-the-century examples from Egypt should, I think, be linked somehow to already long-standing techniques of graphic art in Europe—techniques that, as these original examples show, were just beginning to emerge in the Middle Eastern regions of the Ottoman Empire. Certainly, they reflect features often associated with popular symbolism and the use of folk imagery in various areas of the world around the turn of the century.[3] These features are partially explainable in terms of the limited skills and printing facilities available to the local artists who made them. But it will become apparent that techniques of folk imagery and use of certain easily understood symbols also lent themselves to the challenge of using pictures as tools for political and cultural mobilization among populations that were largely illiterate. Given that literacy was not widespread in early-twentieth-century Egyptian society, the simplicity of such posters held the greatest chance of communicating popular messages—whether specifically political or as reflections of generally shared values—to a broad audience. Consider, for example, figure 0.1 (also reproduced and discussed in some detail in chapter 6 as figure 6.14). It adopts a striking symbol of post–World War I Egyptian nationalists' desire for "Unity of the Nile Valley" through the joined hands of idealized feminine figures (and noble felines) representing Egypt and its former Upper Nile Province of the Sudan.

Once undertaken, this project was bound to raise a question of the uniqueness of the Wafd posters as well as other subjects offered as popular commercial art in the same region in the same period: to what degree do they reflect a locally born artistic product of a particular time and place? Or should we consider the political posters in particular as a local adaptation of an already existing genre? Chapters 3 and 4 suggest that a variety of nineteenth-century models for political caricature art—obvious ones originating in Europe and others, less known, published in India, the Ottoman Empire, and in Egypt itself—were at least theoretically available as sources of inspiration for the lithographs we will be reviewing. But, if one studies examples from the Egyptian commercial graphics market just before and just after World War I for comparison, they share surprisingly few characteristics with most precedents from the late nineteenth century. It is clear that two key themes of political caricature as commonly defined—satire usually combined with humor—held little attraction for creators and buyers of the surviving original lithographs associated with the Wafd political campaign.

Such an absence might be explained in part by the important and widely recognized historical circumstances operating in Egypt when these post–World War I graphics were produced. Thus, chapters 1 and 2 offer an outline of the gradual rise of foreign control followed by imposition of a very firm and formal British protectorate in 1914. We are still left with something of a quandary, however, when one moves beyond the chronologically limited immediate post–World War I period. In fact, once the Wafd's proclaimed goal of achieving independence from British tutelage was at least partially attained in 1923, totally new types of illustrated political satire—often in the form of consciously humorous, and certainly satirical, caricatures—began to emerge as

All Rights Reserved "THE CAIRO PUNCH" Cairo (Egypt)

مصر والسودان ليحي الاستقلال التام لوادي النيل

0.1. Symbolic Unity of the Nile Valley. Courtesy of Lesley Lababidy.

a hallmark of graphics in twentieth-century Egyptian journalism. This is a later development outlined only in general terms in a conclusion that suggests how humorous satirical drawings would become a recognized part of Egyptian popular political culture and journalism by the mid-twentieth century. As they evolved, however, these bore little resemblance to the sober and elementary images used in Egypt's first parliamentary electoral campaign.

Given this shift in later-twentieth-century satirical drawing, are we then considering in the Marriott and Lababidi collections and others a simple historical and/or cultural anomaly? Or are they part of an evolutionary process in artistic expression in Egypt that has escaped attention? One thing is certain: once a journalistic tradition of political caricature took firm root in twentieth-century Egypt, scholarly commentary began and continues to focus on a long succession of cartoonists who embody their own, peculiarly Egyptian, mode of satire and humor in major Cairo and Alexandria newspapers. All commentaries I have examined, however, omit any mention of the quite different (i.e., not at all humorous) precedents that apparently failed to capture the attention of art historians interested in Middle Eastern political caricature.

The noted historian Afaf Lutfi al-Sayyid Marsot set out more than four decades ago to justify, indeed, to insist on, consideration of modern Egyptian *comics* as a *sui generis* product of Egyptian culture.[4] Here, a primary aim is to determine the degree to which a select sampling of early Egyptian political caricatures—not comics per se—reflect not "imported" adaptations of foreign models but original local—or at least regional—creativity. I argue that the artists who drew the Wafd's first posters were following precedents of caricature art—however elementary—that

could be found in the Turkish and Arab regions of the then Ottoman Empire in the years immediately preceding or during World War I. Although Professor Marsot was more concerned with
elements of satire and humor (and therefore "comics") than what appears in the main core of
this book, the discussion will borrow several of her definitions of cartoon (and/or caricature) art.
One definition that will, wherever possible, be applied to the original caricature art reviewed in
this book is her assumption that "the function of any cartoon [and/or caricature] is to influence
the spectator for or against something, either by presenting it as a figure worthy of sympathy,
or by distorting it into a figure of ridicule."[5]

The J. Willard Marriott Library Middle East Library Poster Collection: The Role of Dr. Aziz S. Atiya

Before examining original graphic materials from Egypt and other contemporary regions and
the context within which they were created, it would be well to explain how the collection of rare
Egyptian lithographs came into the possession of the J. Willard Marriott Library.

For more than five decades, starting in 1960, the University of Utah benefitted from a United
States Department of Education grant that helped fund an interdisciplinary Middle East Center involving faculty from several different academic departments. During its earliest years, the
Middle East Center, under the aegis of its first director, Dr. Aziz S. Atiya, laid the bases for a
specialized library that would become, from the early 1960s into the first decade and a half of
the twenty-first century, a nationally and internationally recognized collection of materials in
Middle Eastern and most major Western languages.[6]

The importance of Dr. Atiya's contribution to the development of the Marriott Library's
Middle East holdings prompted the University Board of Regents to name the specialized collection after him in 1964. It was already apparent at that date that the library housed a number
of quite rare original materials purchased by Dr. Atiya during personal trips to the Middle East.
Over the years, valuable acquisitions (most notably a collection of early Egyptian papyri) were
supplemented by several major manuscript and microfilm/microfiche collections, including
more than 900 medieval and early modern manuscripts in Arabic, Hebrew, Persian, and Turkish,
as well as several collections of important private papers.[7] At some point, Dr. Atiya must have
come across the collection of Wafd lithographs among the traditional bookstalls of Ezbakiyya
Square in Cairo or in his dealings with private collectors. He had perhaps more than one reason
for deciding that they deserved a place in the Marriott Library Special Collections' "vault." Those
who knew him recalled later that as a young student in Cairo's School of Medicine he himself
participated in some of the demonstrations that led to the unprecedented political campaign
scenes depicted in the rare original lithographs.[8] Many years after they became part of the Marriott Library collection, I remember how valuable it was as a teacher at the University of Utah
to be able to withdraw several of the original prints from "the vault" to supplement lectures on
the Egyptian nationalist leader Saad Zaghlul and the Wafd movement.

Then, in or around 2004, Dr. Gregory Thompson, now Associate Dean of Special Collections, invited me to produce a "Friends of the Library" brochure, including color reproductions
of selected posters, for distribution to a limited but informed general audience. In stages, key
personalities connected with the library's Middle East collection lent support to the idea of
publishing a more complete study that would place all of the posters in a wider context. Such a
project, it was hoped, could suggest how the posters and other early graphic images in the JWM/
Utah and LL/Cairo collections used symbolism and traditional folk imagery to contribute to
Egypt's early twentieth-century search for a modern national identity.

A stroke of good fortune came several years later when on the occasion of a Special Collections Department exhibition of the posters, Mr. Samir Toubassy, whose successful career as a businessman was then involving him as a Fellow of Harvard University's Advanced Leadership Initiative Program,[9] visited the Middle East Library collection. When he saw the richness of the Library's lithograph collection, Mr. Toubassy became instrumental in providing support, both personal and material, for the efforts that made publication of the current volume possible. The next stage involved working closely with Dr. Greg Thompson, Dr. Leonard Chiarelli, Middle East Collection Librarian, and Dr. John Alley, at that time Editor-in-Chief of the University of Utah Press, to carry the project forward. After John Alley's retirement, Dr. Thomas Krause shouldered responsibilities for the final preparation of the manuscript. Dr. Judy Jarrow of the Special Collections staff read the first rough draft of the manuscript and provided important additional contributions.

The author was able to benefit from the published work and personal suggestions from a limited handful of researchers familiar with early graphics printed in Egypt. However, because even specialists were unaware of the existence of lithograph posters such as those in the Marriott Library, it was difficult to uncover clues concerning the probable provenance of the early Wafd posters and the artistic style they reflected. When the particular importance of an Egyptian illustrator who founded the satirical illustrated journal *al-Siyâsah al-muṣawwara* (a.k.a. the *Cairo Punch*, in 1907) became apparent, the need to draw on the extensive knowledge of Oxford University Professor Marilyn Booth became critical. Professor Booth kindly responded to inquiries concerning her work with the earliest issues of the *Cairo Punch* held by the Hoover Institution at Stanford University. Her response to my suggestion that the publisher of the *Cairo Punch* played a seminal role in an up-to-now unknown post–World War I period of original political caricature art in Egypt confirmed my view: the Wafd campaign posters deserve attention as a contribution, however modest, to the political and art history of the modern Middle East.[10]

The content of this book has undergone several stages of reorganization since the first exploratory draft. It was clear that, even though a main goal was to build an argument concerning the provenance and then the "fate" of these early Egyptian graphics, any reader would need some idea of the already special position of Egypt in modern Middle Eastern history from the nineteenth into the twentieth century. Thus, since the Wafd poster collection openly proclaims Egypt's need for *istiqlâl tammâm*, or "complete independence" from Great Britain after 1918, I ask the general reader to be patient as chapter 1 provides an overview of how a province of the Ottoman Empire came to be separated in the nineteenth century, only to fall under British protection.

Since the post-1918 call for Egypt's independence was sounded by an initially rather conservative politician turned intransigent nationalist leader—Saad Zaghlul Pasha—chapter 2 provides general biographical information concerning the man who appears prominently in almost all the surviving political campaign posters. Readers already familiar with these critical years of Egyptian history may wish to proceed to the two chapters surveying earlier "models." First comes a summary review of obviously well-known nineteenth-century caricature art in Europe (chapter 3). Then the same interpretive themes introduced there—symbolism in caricatures and folk imagery—are used to discuss examples of pre-1914 political caricature from non-European areas—India, the Ottoman Empire, and then Egypt itself (chapter 4). Although it appears that such non-European precedents did not actually inspire the artists who produced the Wafd posters, they do offer a useful framework for comparison with the art forms adopted in support of Saad Zaghlul.

Chapter 5 deals with a variety of original lithographs that may in fact have had some bearing on the styles used by the artists who drew the Wafd posters. A main figure here—the founder of the *Cairo Punch*, introduced above—actually participated in *all* of the domains of caricature art pertinent to our discussion, passing from political satire, through totally nonsatirical political propaganda, to "popular" commercial posters distributed for sale in Egypt in the pre-1914 period. Together with a number of lesser known local artists, the same individual eventually played a key role in publishing the posters that openly adopted symbolism and Egyptian folk imagery in the Wafd's cause.

Nearly thirty of these rare original posters supporting the Wafd are then reviewed under a variety of rubrics. Chapter 6 opens with a review of portraits of Egyptian personalities appearing symbolically in posters dominated by Saad Zaghlul. It then goes on to interpret elements of symbolism and folk imagery in a variety of different contemporary posters. These clearly reflected—in quite elementary form—social and cultural values, including gender issues and urban-rural relationships, that the Wafd sought to interject indirectly into its inaugural political campaign.

Finally, a brief conclusion raises the question of the evolving characteristics of caricature art in Egypt in the next several generations after the focal period that followed World War I. The forms of satire and humor that emerged in these later years and became emblematic of Egyptian political caricatures for the rest of the century make it difficult to remember that totally different perceptions of the role of graphics in politics held sway—if only for a short time—in the print shops of Cairo and Alexandria.

1

GENERAL EGYPTIAN HISTORICAL BACKGROUND TO 1914

Egypt's experiences in the periods before and after World War I help place the founding of the Wafd Party and the related posters in broader historical context. But what happened during the war itself in the short period of 1914–1918 was actually the culmination of a long process, one that began a century before, when quite distant events began shaping subsequent stages of modern Middle East and Egyptian history. Many regional and even global events would make Egypt an important entity on its own, quite different from its eastern Mediterranean neighbors.

By the end of the last full century of Ottoman imperial rule over the Middle East, Egypt came to be occupied by Britain following tumultuous events that unfolded between 1879 and 1882. This turning point in Middle East history would be followed by further stages of Ottoman decline, stages that ended with defeat of the empire at the end of World War I. After 1918 came a series of political settlements that left most of the region divided into mandatory regimes assigned by the League of Nations to Britain and France in the Levant and Iraq. Egypt remained until 1922 under a formal protectorate regime that had been declared by Britain during the War.[1]

Egypt as an Ottoman Province before 1850

Egypt was one of several pashaliks, or provinces of the Ottoman Empire, that would experience rising European interference in their internal governance after the 1850s. As World War I and the end of the Ottoman Empire approached, the entire Middle East was poised for indirect foreign control. Because of the particular circumstances that forged Egypt's history along lines that differed from those of its neighboring provinces Syria and Iraq during the nineteenth century, Egypt entered the wartime years with a totally distinct "legal" status in international law. This took the form of a formal protectorate: a presumed bilateral treaty that Britain considered part of her own sovereign authority. Egypt came out of the war, therefore, under conditions that the League of Nations was forced to recognize as unlike those affecting other former Ottoman provinces.

A brief review of how those conditions came about will explain why, when the League established the new precedent of temporary mandate authorities (France in Greater Syria, and Britain in Iraq and Palestine), Egypt's emerging interwar nationalist experience would necessarily be unique.

In fact, already in the first quarter of the nineteenth century the course of Egypt's history as an Ottoman province bore very distinct marks. As the century unfolded, those differences became more pronounced until, for better or for worse, the sultanate was forced to recognize that its authority over Egypt had become purely symbolic.

The Ottoman pashalik of Egypt was just recovering from the effects of occupation between 1798 and 1802 by French troops under Napoleon Bonaparte when it came under the strong-arm control of a different type of Ottoman governor: Muhammad 'Ali Pasha (r. 1805–1848).[2] The French occupation effectively removed inefficient rule by Mamluk military potentates who had, for more than a century, paid little heed to Ottoman claims to govern the province. Muhammad 'Ali completed the French task, ostensibly in order to restore Ottoman authority. But soon it became evident that he wished to lay the bases for his own autocratic rule in Egypt. Between 1811, when the last Mamluks were eradicated by force, and the mid-1820s, when Muhammad 'Ali assisted the sultan in repressing insurrectionists in Greece, his moves centered on building a provincial military system under his own control. At the same time, he restructured fiscal and agricultural production methods to guarantee the economic means to carry out his military reforms. Despite Muhammad 'Ali's show of loyalty to Istanbul during the Greek rebellion, the effort fell short of the sultan's hopes, not because of a lack of effective military help from Egypt, but because the Concert of Europe launched its first post-Napoleonic move to intervene in Ottoman affairs. This move led to the diplomatic maneuverings that brought Greece's independence within a few years.

Such setbacks marked a new stage in relations between Cairo and Istanbul. While the sultanate of Mahmud II (r. 1808–1839) struggled to reforge its declining military and administrative system, Muhammad 'Ali continued to strengthen his hold over his own army and Egypt's political and economic affairs. He used monopolistic agricultural controls, especially for Nile Valley cotton, which was becoming increasingly important as a cash crop that could build up Egypt's treasury. For a variety of reasons, but mainly to increase his own importance throughout the region, Muhammad 'Ali (more exactly his son Ibrahim) advanced in 1831 into the adjacent Ottoman province of Syria. One pretext was to serve Mahmud's goal of restructuring outmoded Ottoman methods of governance in Syria. Application of the same monopolistic economic controls used in Egypt (coupled with Ibrahim's forced militarization of both central and local political controls in Syria), however, led to an open break with the sultan's representatives and another military advance by Egypt in 1839, this time deep into the Anatolian core of the empire.

These tumultuous events caused the Concert of Europe to threaten intervention in the Levant. High-level diplomacy, however, secured Muhammad 'Ali's withdrawal from Syria and a promise to reduce Egypt's military forces. In return, a major concession changed the course of Egypt's history for more than a century: an Imperial Firman in 1841 granted the (unprecedented) hereditary right of succession to Egypt's governorate to the family of Muhammad 'Ali. Thus, in the last few years of Muhammad 'Ali's rule, the stage was set for attempting new, though militarily less spectacular, paths to de facto Egyptian autonomy within the declining Ottoman Empire.

A series of landmarks along this road, some quite well known and others familiar mainly to specialists of Egyptian history, would lead to the transfer of interventionist prerogatives from

Istanbul to several European capitals and, quite dramatically, to British military occupation in 1882.

Muhammad ʿAli's Successors: Provincial Autonomy at a Cost, 1854–1879

Between 1850 and the mid-1870s, Muhammad ʿAli's successors were unable to exercise the same degree of control he had used to enforce centralized military and administrative reforms particular to Egypt. His second successor (and fourth son), Said (r. 1854–1863), however, charted one major new direction that promised to make Egypt a "showcase" attracting worldwide attention. Said's original grant of a concession (to Ferdinand de Lesseps's privately subscribed *Compagnie Universelle du Canal Maritime de Suez*) to build the Suez Canal only produced concrete results when work was finally completed under the second son of Ibrahim Pasha, Ismaʿil (r. 1863–1879). A key to understanding why Egypt was beginning to experience new forms of external pressure when the Canal opened in 1869 lay in financial precedents that followed the original concession. What began during the cotton export boom years of the mid-1860s as plans to expand canal usage led to serious deficit spending for facilities such as rail connections and extensive port facilities in Port Said and Alexandria. Deficits widened when Ismaʿil disbursed large amounts of money for many unwise projects, including construction of palatial residences for himself and his family. Such spending was precariously supported by various forms of borrowing, including public bonds (almost all purchased by private foreign investors) and loans obtained from European banking houses.[3] Foreign powers viewed such unprecedented dealings with concern, anticipating difficulties should their nationals (or nationals of rival countries) seek diplomatic intervention to protect their interests as creditors.

Ismaʿil, however, negotiated several agreements with the Ottoman Sultanate that allowed him to continue increasing Egypt's level of debt. The assumption that Egypt's provincial treasury would be separately responsible for meeting such obligations was accompanied by another (mainly symbolic) grant of distinct status to the hereditary governorate earlier obtained by Muhammad ʿAli: Ismaʿil received the unique title Khedive of Egypt. The title was passed on to his successors until the charade of Egyptian autonomy within the Ottoman Empire was cancelled under totally changed circumstances. These circumstances began with foreign occupation in 1882 and culminated with World War I, when Britain deposed the last khedive and created a "new" sultanate in Egypt bound by a bilateral protectorate treaty.

Growing European Intervention

Egypt's indebtedness became even worse during the first decade of Suez Canal operations. This led to more borrowing at higher rates and a number of extraordinary arrangements meant to insure foreign governments and foreign lenders against looming fears of khedival bankruptcy. Several unparalleled institutions run by *private* foreigners representing creditors, including the foreign-staffed Public Debt Commission and the French and British Dual Control, were created. In 1875, another capitulatory, or extraterritorial, addition was a foreign-majority system of mixed courts to judge civil and commercial matters in which any single party was a national of the several countries then enjoying extraterritorial privileges recognized by treaties with the Ottoman Empire.[4]

Things came to a breaking point in 1879, four years after Prime Minister Benjamin Disraeli used British treasury funds to buy shares that made the British government the largest holder of capital in the Suez Canal Company.[5] In 1878, a specially appointed international commission of inquiry had reported that unless drastic internal fiscal and administrative reform measures were taken Egypt would have to declare bankruptcy, causing losses by foreign creditors and a likely plummeting of Canal share values. Isma'il's reaction led to a first crisis over what supporters of Egypt's presumed autonomous fiscal and legislative status thought should be the only authority to settle such issues: a locally elected, legislatively responsible Egyptian Council of Representatives (*majlis al-nuwwâb*). Inevitable clashes between representatives of foreign holders of Egypt's debt obligations and a first ill-fated Majlis ended in high-level (mainly British and French ambassadorial) intervention in Istanbul and the deposition of Khedive Isma'il. This was coupled with closure of the Majlis in May 1879.[6]

Isma'il's successor, Tawfiq (r. 1879–1892), was obliged to accept even more overt forms of foreign financial and political supervision after the first Majlis crisis. These only added to the unsettled conditions, which in turn led to the sudden British decision to send troops to occupy Egypt in 1882. The move was supposedly undertaken in the name of all international parties concerned by the Egyptian crisis—including the presumed sovereign authority of the sultan in Istanbul.

In fact, soon after assuming the khedivate, Tawfiq found himself trapped between the unsatisfied aspirations of local supporters of the abortive Majlis movement and foreign interests that insisted reforms should be pushed through under the guidance of special, foreign-controlled agencies. Resentment of such foreign pressures, especially calls for budgetary cuts and "redirection" of scarce funds to service the debt, began to be aired in different Egyptian circles. Such circles ranged from disgruntled landowners fearing unfavorable changes in their tax status to unpaid government employees. Most important for the rising radical support for Egyptian legislative and budgetary autonomy under a restored Majlis, middle ranking army officers—many unpaid—rallied around an unexpected but vocal leader, Colonel Ahmad 'Urabi. 'Urabi soon made demands that foreign governments intent on protecting the interests of their own nationals, as well as those with credit claims, found unacceptable. Although direct connections are not fully documented, the defenders of nascent Egyptian "nationalist" demands include several very major figures in Middle Eastern cultural and intellectual history, such as Jamal al-Din al-Afghani and Shaykh Muhammad 'Abduh, both of whom supported 'Urabi's call to free Egypt from growing outside control. By 1881, rising tensions were evident in several local journalistic organs, some mirroring Islamic conservative undertones, defending what was perceived as the Egyptian "fatherland," or *watan*.

In fact, however, when the foreign diplomatic community acceded cautiously to local demands for a newly elected Majlis at the end of 1881, those who hoped to see the return of a moderate majority were disappointed. "Watanist" enthusiasm predominated as a cabinet including Colonel 'Urabi as defense minister supported legislative pronouncements reversing reform measures put in place under (British and French-sponsored) Dual Control aegis during the previous several years.

Whether the decision to send a British military expedition to Egypt (initially intended to be an Anglo-French force acting in behalf of all governments with a stake in the "Egyptian Question") was a reaction to the radical political and legislative stand of the Majlis of 1882, or, as claimed by Gladstone's government, primarily to quell rising violence against foreigners and their property, the British occupation of Egypt took place rapidly during the early summer of 1882. In the immediate aftermath, most other European capitals applauded strong actions against Egyptian political and military resistance to Britain's fait accompli. Support for the "temporary" occupation, however, was based on the assumption that action had been taken in the interest of all foreign parties and that responsibility for what was to come would be shared among members of the international community. Such expectations would fade as the first and subsequent stages of the occupation regime took form. But what is most important for understanding the ensuing events as one decade of British control followed another is not just the fictional international-ization of the Egyptian Question. Rather, it is the way in which Egyptians at different levels of society were led by the experience of British occupation to form views of what best fit Egypt's presumed national interests conjunct with their own individual identities.

The process that led to such views was of course much more complex than what is suggested in the limited scope of this book. Still, interesting symbols of this experience could be and were eventually expressed in graphic form. Documentation of the remnants of such graphics, like written evidence, can help forge linkages between historical facts of this earlier period and later popularly accepted representations of the same.

Early British Occupation Policies

The thirty-two-year period of Britain's occupation of Egypt before World War I produced many rationalizations to justify policies supporting Britain's key interests in Egypt and in the Otto-man region generally. Particularly in the early years after 1882, London faced strong criticism of claims that its actions were solely intended to stabilize financial and fiscal matters, soon to be followed by return to the *status quo ante*. Countries jealous of Britain's paramount position in Egypt, especially France, tried every means possible to keep London from benefitting from what could become a de facto colonial advantage. Typical measures used by the French (and other countries with substantial private and political interests in Egypt, including Greece and Italy) involved bids for appointments for their nationals in key administrations with budgets linked to the still looming public debt. Paris insisted on maintaining a privileged presence in Egypt's mixed courts and claimed prestigious appointments such as the directorships of the Khedival School of Law and the emerging nucleus of what would become the world-famous Egyptian National Museum. Both of these were headed by French appointees throughout the Occupation.

All of this contributed to the impression among informed sectors of Egyptian society of the time that, no matter what methods for personal advancement might be attempted—either through higher education via the limited possibilities available, or the patronage of tradition-ally influential "notable" and wealthy families—there was little hope of overcoming privileges enjoyed by the foreign resident community and the network of controls held by the occupying power. This impression grew as the years passed, particularly among a cadre of educated Egyp-tians who considered themselves qualified to participate in political decision-making. Especially concerned were Egyptians who had received a European form of education and were willing to adopt certain aspects of Western culture. Mirrored across the Ottoman Empire, such groups were increasingly being labeled effendis.[7]

Yet it took more than two decades and a considerably changed occupation regime before a promised Egyptian legislative assembly was temporarily activated to accommodate some level of local political participation in the decision-making process. Among the early participants in that concessionary move would be, at least until 1918, Wafd founder Saad Zaghlul. It remains something of a mystery how Zaghlul's role in this earlier period shifted after 1918 to a strong anti-British stance with Wafdist slogans (but apparently not yet graphics) previously unthinkable, directly challenging the "temporary" British occupation.

In fact, entering the first decade of the twentieth century, effendi figures like Saad Zaghlul and others still sought the confidence of occupation authorities continued to feel they could lead a movement for Egypt's independence without resorting to extremism. Such aspirations were, however, still far from being defined in the period between 1882 and the turn of the new century. Not only were there few Egyptian candidates for serious political responsibilities, but into the 1890s, London still faced opposition from foreign rivals to any moves that might gain unilateral advantages for Britain in a post-occupation setting.[8]

Meanwhile, the man who had begun as a privately appointed British member of the international Public Debt Commission, Sir Evelyn Baring (later Lord Cromer), was bent on obtaining practical results no matter what obstacles foreign or Egyptian opponents might put in the way. Baring was appointed to the key post of British Agent and Consul General in 1883 and served in this status for nearly twenty-five years. His title (but clearly not his determined assumption of wide-ranging responsibilities) was a holdover from the pre-occupation fiction that foreign diplomatic representatives in Egypt had consular authority only. Full official responsibilities were assumed to rest with ambassadors to Istanbul. In reality, Baring began from the outset to manage all local aspects of occupation policy in direct communication with the Foreign Secretary in London.[9] To assure local "cooperation," the British recognized an Egyptian cabinet whose prime minister headed several ministries. In addition, there was an even less politically influential, individually appointed Legislative Council.

Maneuvers for local political influence, mainly through the office of prime minister, represented the most dramatic challenges for British policy during the first years of the occupation. The details of appointments and dismissals of prime ministers between 1883 and 1892, the year of Khedive Tawfiq's death and the accession of Abbas II (r. 1892–1914), are less important here than a key question: what was the traditional social, economic, and cultural milieu within which contests for British approval of high-level posts took place? In fact, all three men who headed Egyptian cabinets before 1893 came from families that had achieved traditional elite status before the British occupation. All three had served briefly as prime minister in the "troubled times" between 1878 and 1882. Most important, *none* bore the characteristics of the emerging "middle class" *affandiyya*.

Although quite different in their personal attributes, Muhammad Sharif Pasha, Nubar Pasha, and Mustafa Riyadh Pasha, were all independently wealthy (mainly because of family landholdings). Of the three, Nubar, whose family was of Armenian descent with branches throughout the Levant, and Muhammad Sharif, a highly placed descendant of families then referred to as Turco-Circassians (Turkish-speaking elite immigrants who lent support to Muhammad 'Ali during the first half of the century), had cultivated some form of privileged interaction with Western "sponsors." This would either have been through Levantine trading networks (the experience of Nubar's family) or through links established while engaged in education abroad—the case of Muhammad Sharif.[10] Mustafa Riyadh, also of Turco-Circassian origin, was probably the most firmly rooted in the conservative network of influential landowners in the Egyptian provinces.

Each may have counted on particular aspects of his background to attract British support for his candidacy to lead the cabinet. Sharif had formed (but failed in) a pre-occupation cabinet under a presumed banner of support for a moderate, autonomous representative legislature. He gained early backing (and the prime ministership in 1883) from British Foreign Secretary Lord Granville. Sharif's definitive departure (after opposing London's abandonment of Egypt's claim to sovereignty over the Sudan—later a theme reappearing quite prominently in the Wafd's campaign posters linking the two Nilotic regions) meant that families whose material, social, and political welfare somehow depended on his patronage would have had to adjust their sights accordingly.[11]

In Nubar Pasha's case, his service as prime minister (especially between 1885 and 1888) was underpinned by the hope that his wide experience in dealing with capitulatory questions would speed replacement of the foreign-dominated mixed judiciary with "true" Egyptian *ahliyya*, or "native" courts.[12] Here again, however, Nubar's desire to follow his own political priorities led to repeated fallings out with the occupation authorities.

After each stalemate over the prime ministership, Mustafa Riyadh, arch rival of Nubar, could be counted on to put forward his candidacy and assumed willingness to follow British occupation priorities. Such assumptions lasted until Riyadh also clashed with Baring and London over increased British influence in the form of occupation advisers to two key ministries in 1892.

Policy Changes in the 1890s and the First Nationalist Watan Movement in 1907

Evelyn Baring's confrontation with Mustafa Riyadh came in the same year as the death of Taw-fiq and accession of the last Khedive, Abbas II (r. 1892–1914).[13] From 1892 until 1907, London imposed supervisory controls in a number of new areas. Whether a reflection of acceptance of the inevitable necessity of Britain's staying in Egypt for geostrategic reasons or recognition that the system in place by the mid-1890s was proving to be effective, most observers—whether foreign or Egyptian—saw little likelihood of change in the status quo. An example of this modus operandi came in the choice of Egyptian notable figures such as Mustafa Fahmi Pasha (1840–1914) to fill high posts that gained them public recognition, even though they had minor roles in key decision-making processes.[14] At the same time, few signs of dissatisfaction seemed to be appearing, especially among groups who, through education or more recent family material accomplishments, might be tempted to organize some new form of anti-occupation activity. This remark is particularly important given the fact that, as signs of change surfaced in late 1890s, a number of aspirants to offices depending on indirect British sponsorship (including the future founder of the post-1918 Wafd movement himself) remained relatively undisturbed. This held true even when voices of discontent emerged that would be associated with the first serious signs of Egyptian nationalism a number of years before World War I.

Somewhat ironically, a sequence of events often cited as the starting point of new opposition to Britain in Egypt actually began as part of the emerging rivalry between the British and the French over spheres of influence in Africa. By the late 1890s, this rivalry was pushing London and Paris to the brink of open conflict over strategic access to the Upper (White) Nile zone, symbolized by the otherwise little-known Shilluk tribal ceremonial town of Fashoda. To guarantee that French expeditionary columns headed toward Fashoda would not succeed in firming up France's reach from West Africa (where it already had established claims), a latter-day decision was made in 1898 to send Anglo-Egyptian military forces to reacquire Sudanese territories lost to the break-away Mahdist movement more than a decade earlier. When this was accomplished under the forceful command of Sir Herbert Kitchener, the question of the future disposition of Egypt's former Sudanese territories was inevitably catapulted to the forefront of international politics.

The reacquired Sudan also provided fuel for Egyptian critics of what became Britain's 1899 fait accompli—imposition of an Anglo-Egyptian Condominium *separate* from the occupation administration in Egypt. Although this proved to be a false start, a movement headed by the young French-trained lawyer Mustafa Kamil (the same Mustafa Kamil who would figure posthumously—like Shaykh Muhammad 'Abduh and Jamal al-Din al-Afghani—in Wafd propaganda posters two decades later) tried to use the issue to rally opposition to Britain's occupation strategy.[15]

A second major incident, also involving questions of international borders and Mustafa Kamil's by-then expanding Watan (Fatherland) movement, occurred in 1906. The nascent Egyptian opposition press tied to Kamil's "party" organ, *al-Liwâ* (*the Banner*), again sought popular support for its denunciation of British moves to serve its own geopolitical ends in the so-called "Taba incident." Like the Sudan Condominium issue, however, the Taba incident involved complexities of international law well beyond the ken of common Egyptians. It occurred, and was soon over, when the British sent troops to force Turkish occupants out of Taba, an Egyptian town near Aqaba, the small port at the head of the strategically important Gulf of Aqaba. An Anglo-Ottoman compromise was soon reached by ceding a nondescript stretch of land that was traditionally Egyptian to symbolically allow the Ottomans Red Sea access, while Taba itself remained under "Egypt's" control. Occupation authorities subsequently registered a certain level of alarm over the position of Kamil's Watan press, which supported Ottoman claims *against* the British. But by then London was reassured of a relatively free hand in Egypt following its 1904 Entente Cordiale with France. Thus, no consequence comparable to earlier and continuing international concerns over the Sudan followed.[16]

More important for the emergent Watanists' bid to speak, not only for Egypt's educated and informed minority but for thousands of common Egyptians, was the notorious Denshawai affair. This case involved the sentencing to hanging of several Denshawai villagers for assaulting British officers hunting pigeons on their land without permission. These draconian judgments were handed down by a military court without even considering hearings through the twenty-five-year-old European model *ahliyya* courts that had been sponsored by the British themselves. The Denshawai scandal appeared later in graphic illustrations printed by anti-British publishers seeking to bring Mustafa Kamil's cause before the Egyptian public. One of these, published by the same press that eventually pioneered—in a totally different graphic style—post–World War I support for Saad Zaghlul's Wafd, bore the personal mark of *Cairo Punch* editor 'Abd al-Hamid Zaki.[17]

What is important for this brief historical survey is the fact that, although the grim symbol of Denshawai was raised in 1906 as a simple, but highly controversial popular cause, the vehicle for its dissemination at that time was still limited to print. Such a medium, even when it tried to mobilize opinion around controversial popular causes, had little chance of reaching illiterate Egyptians unless read aloud by "volunteer" subscribers.

The Post–Kamil Hiatus: Political Compromises in 1914 and World War I

Although Mustafa Kamil died at an early age in 1908, the movement he fostered continued well into the twentieth century. Yet almost all signs point to the fact that neither of his two immediate successors, as presumed leaders of the Watan group, showed signs of wanting to transfer their political loyalties to the Wafd when it launched its own bid for Egyptian independence in 1918. This was true even though the Wafd, when it emerged, clearly supported much the same goal: denunciation of British control over Egypt. Thus, as part of the Wafd's search for useful popular symbols, all three pre-1914 Watan figures would be "adopted," not just once but frequently in its poster campaign supporting Saad Zaghlul. Ironically, then, all three of Zaghlul's prewar Watanist predecessors, none of whom were ever members of the Wafd—Kamil himself, Muhammad Farid, and Shaykh 'Abd al-'Aziz Shawish—continued to hold central symbolic positions that Zaghlul had to recognize whether he wanted to or not.[18] The dominant symbol of his sole leadership would only be attainable in stages, several years in fact after the Wafd movement's cause was declared in 1918.

In all events, between Mustafa Kamil's death in 1908 and the outbreak of World War I, several general features of the occupation regime were undergoing changes. Had it not been for the coming of the war, signs of evolutionary change—and therefore expectations of gradual improvement for both the masses of the Egyptian population and the educated minority—tended to outweigh the likelihood that controversial incidents such as Denshawai would again push the situation toward open confrontation.

New directions surfaced after the retirement of Lord Cromer in 1907 and his replacement by Sir Eldon Gorst, who arrived with considerable earlier experience as adviser to two Egyptian ministries.[19] Following Gorst's death in 1911, the last figure to fill the Consul General's post before the shift to a wartime protectorate was Sir Herbert Kitchener, former adviser in the ministry of the interior and military commander of the 1897–1898 Sudan campaign.[20]

The seven-year period between 1907 and 1914, especially during Kitchener's tenure, showed continuing progress toward the often-repeated goal of improving local administration and fiscal and financial stability. For Egyptians who aspired to government service and an actual role in political and legislative matters, Kitchener made plans to introduce a long-awaited *elected* Legislative Assembly. Such directions probably encouraged what some political aspirants and favored elites—most notably the founders of the *Hizb al-Umma* (Party of the People [or Community]) movement and its moderately nationalist newspaper *al-Jarîda*, founded in 1907—preferred over the confrontational issues that had been Mustafa Kamil's hallmark.[21]

Meanwhile, at each stage leading up to 1914, Saad Zaghlul, future founder of the Wafd, vied for recognized status among his Egyptian peers. The same peers vied among themselves for paths to advancement that continued to depend on various forms of British sponsorship. Events accompanying the outbreak of World War I changed this situation.

THE CAREER OF SAAD ZAGHLUL PASHA AND EARLY POSTWAR WAFD POLITICS

In Egypt's complex prewar environment, Saad Zaghlul progressed from modest rural origin in the pre-British occupation period to become a prominent politician at the outbreak of World War I. If, by that date, he had any inclination to join a group associated with an identifiable political program, it probably would have been the moderately nationalist, "evolutionary" *Hizb al-Umma*.

Four years later, however, Zaghlul suddenly announced the formation under his leadership of what appeared to be the openly defiant *Hizb al-Wafd al-Misri,* the Egyptian Delegation Party. Once this movement gained the forefront at the expense of "old-guard" politicians as well as hopefuls looking to the Watan or Umma Parties, Zaghlul went on to forge what became—despite repeated and controversial setbacks—Egypt's best-known nationalist party for the next three and a half decades. It was this group that used the lithographic posters that form the subject of this book—with their many historical symbols and folk images—to claim leadership of Egypt's bid for full independence from British control.

Zaghlul's Early Career

There is no reason here to discuss all details of Zaghlul's career before he became prime minister at the head of Egypt's first elected parliament in 1924. The main lines of his life may suggest why early Wafdists supported his candidacy in the parliamentary election campaign of 1923. They do not, however, necessarily clarify why the graphics accompanying that campaign took on the particular artistic forms that became their hallmark.

Saad Zaghlul was born in 1859 to a traditionally well-established peasant family in the Kafr al-Shaykh district of the western Nile Delta. By the late 1870s, he began (but did not finish) studies at al-Azhar, the internationally prestigious center of Islamic learning in Cairo. His first position of employment was with Egypt's official journal, *al-Waqāʾiʿ al-miṣriyya*.[1] From there he moved to a middle-level appointment in the legal department of the Ministry of the Interior. Recognizing the limitations of mere administrative functions, he decided to pursue the study of European law locally in Cairo. Not all Egyptian students seeking law diplomas at this time were members of the well-to-do elite class. The more or less privileged students whose families could not afford to send them to European universities joined "middle-class" students (perhaps the case of Saad Zaghlul) to seek training in schools such as the recently founded Khedival Law School, the French-funded private law school, or another lesser-known local alternative. Many of these students earned places of importance in the poster campaign mounted in the name of the Wafd. Together, they progressed from relative anonymity to visible prominence as hopeful political figures just before and after World War I.

Yet there is no reason to suggest that early currents of political activism were already taking preliminary form when Zaghlul became interested in a law career. Possibly by the time Mustafa Kamil pursued his study of law in the mid-1890s, however, the linkage between "modern" legal training and politics was beginning to play a role unknown when Zaghlul trained as a lawyer.

A certain irony attaches to the eventual careers of these two individuals and their choice of a legal profession. First, the young and flamboyant Kamil went on to study law at the University of Toulouse in France—an experience that probably contributed to his reputation (unlike Zaghlul) as a Europhile. Historians dealing with the Watan movement tend to link this attribute with various signs that Kamil's nationalist politics (also unlike Zaghlul) sometimes depended on garnering support from parties outside Egypt.[2] A second, more obvious irony is that the younger Kamil *preceded* Zaghlul as a controversial champion of anti-British nationalism well before the latter even began to veer from the security of the career that lay before him once he completed his legal training.

In fact, once Zaghlul completed his studies his career advanced pragmatically from private practice to increasingly higher levels of recognition of his capacities as a jurist. In 1892 (the year in which the first formal British judicial adviser was appointed over vocal Egyptian opposition), he received a judgeship in the decade-old "native," or *ahliyya* courts.

By this date, in part because of his rapid professional advancement, Zaghlul was becoming well known in the higher levels of Cairo society, giving him contacts with individuals who, often owing to their families' high standing or wealth, held important, if largely symbolic, political positions. Probably the most important among these was Mustafa Fahmi Pasha (1840–1914), a retired military officer born in Algeria in a family with Ottoman Turkish background. Immigrating from French-controlled Algeria before the occupation, Fahmi quickly rose to prominence, first as governor of several Egyptian provinces including the key maritime zone of Port Said. By 1879, he was minister of public works. In the early years of the occupation, he gained the confidence of the British, who agreed to his appointment to several important ministries. After the reshuffling of political priorities that followed the death of Khedive Tawfiq in 1892, Fahmi's candidacy for top political posts may at first have served a convenient interim need. But, after serving a first time as prime minister, his importance as a stabilizing force transformed his interim status into a long-term political arrangement. Fahmi stayed on as prime minister for thirteen years from the end of 1895 to November 1908—sufficient time to form a political network that would be welcomed by some but perhaps resented by others. That this move toward moderate elite leadership was appreciated by Saad Zaghlul would become apparent both in terms of personal relationships and political opportunities that helped open several doors for Zaghlul at least until 1914.

In 1896, just as Fahmi began his second and very long tenure as head of the Egyptian cabinet, Saad Zaghlul, then age thirty-seven, married Fahmi's twenty-year-old daughter, Safiya. The importance of this union between a representative of the rising Egyptian effendi class who had become a prominent jurist and an obviously privileged descendant of a wealthy Turco-Circassian family became increasingly evident as the years passed.[3]

Zaghlul's legal career prospered in the decade that followed his marriage, earning him his first political appointment in 1906 as Minister of Education (1906–1908) and a second post (after his father-in-law retired) as Minister of Justice (1910–1912).

Compromise with Political Moderates before Declaration of the Protectorate in 1914

Having achieved widely respected status, Zaghlul had reason to look forward to continued advancement, even if this meant working within the accepted boundaries of the occupation regime. Indeed, such hopes were further kindled by the policies of Herbert Kitchener, whose support for wider legislative representation by qualified Egyptians was mentioned earlier. Zaghlul was definitely among those who could expect to receive such recognition. In 1913, he was elected to serve as vice president of a new legislative body scheduled for inauguration the following year.

Such prospects clearly responded to the gradualist expectations of moderates who supported Umma Party candidates, mainly to counter openly nationalist and anti-British "holdovers" from Mustafa Kamil's Watan Party. Two such individuals, Kamil's successor as party head, Muham-mad Bey Farid, and his fiery associate, Shaykh ʿAbd al-ʿAziz Shawish, had already been declared *personae non grata* in 1911 and were living in exile in Istanbul.[4]

The outbreak of World War I in 1914 and the Ottoman Empire's fateful decision to join the Central Powers brought the single most important change in British policy toward Egypt since 1882. In December 1914, London essentially imposed a formal protectorate regime—achieved only after deposing Abbas II and naming the son of Khedive Ismaʿil, Husayn Kamil (1853–1917), to fill the "new" and unilaterally created position of Sultan of Egypt. This ended the convenient fiction that London was exercising its role of benevolent occupier in the name of Istanbul. Brit-ain's obvious need to protect the Suez Canal from Ottoman military advances soon led to sharp increases in troop numbers and auxiliary forces in Egypt. There was also an emergency increase in responsibility for British advisers in all branches of the Egyptian government. All local pro-tectorate authority was to be exercised by a High Commissioner named directly by the Foreign Office. The first high commissioner was Sir Henry McMahon, replaced by Sir Reginald Wingate at the end of 1916. For his part, Wingate was destined to exercise an ultimately unsuccessful role trying to define a "favorable" political path for Zaghlul and other political hopefuls as the pro-tectorate regime moved from year to year during the war.

Since the war was the High Commissioner's main priority during 1914 and 1915, measures earlier extended to Egyptian political aspirants—especially elections for a new legislative assem-bly—were placed on hold. Instead of political reform, strict economic controls and wholesale requisitioning of manpower would take precedence over the next few years. Historians frequently cite the effect of increasingly heavy economic and fiscal controls as a primary factor behind the tumultuous demonstrations that shook Egypt at the end of the war. The demonstrations came just as the first self-proclaimed Wafd headed by Saad Zaghlul launched its call for an immediate end to the "emergency" protectorate regime and full independence. A number of studies of the 1914–1918 period recognize that the demonstrations rose spontaneously in response to the disruptive effects of wartime demands and conditions.[5] That the sudden announcement of the Wafd's uncompromising political demands should have been taken up as part and parcel of such popular grievances is, however, only partly explainable in the same terms.

Political Disappointments before the 1918 Armistice: Key to the Wafd's "New" Movement?

Different potential Egyptian political leaders vied rather openly for positions in the wartime protectorate cabinet. This admittedly summary account suggests that such rivalries forced Saad Zaghlul to maneuver carefully to keep from losing the political ground he had gained since 1907. Perhaps, even, his unprecedented self-assigned mandate to speak for the totality of the Egyptian people once the war ended was a tactic to escape the personal intrigues of several rivals. One way to achieve this goal would have been to capitalize on the widespread discontent of the masses, using easily understood popular symbols, regardless of whether all parties sufficiently understood the high-level technicalities involved. Perhaps it is in this light that we should consider the Wafd's "sudden" recognition of the importance of using graphic images based on elementary caricature and folk imagery.

The formal British protectorate after 1914 was bound to affect any Egyptians who had begun to plan their future around a gradual loosening of occupation controls. For political hopefuls, a new set of potential stakes definitely took form by the last year or so of World War I. These stakes undoubtedly played a role in shifting Saad Zaghlul's accommodating stance toward his former (indirect) British patrons to one that challenged the protectorate as well as the conveniently created figurehead of Sultan Husayn Kamil. Judging from the time-tested history of the early Wafd by Janice Terry, it appears that, after the first few years of the wartime protectorate, Zaghlul had several occasions to conclude that he was more vulnerable now than in his previous years of predictable political advancement.[6]

The first sign that Zaghlul would have to be wary of new forms of political maneuvering under the protectorate came after the death of Husayn Kamil in 1917, when the new sultan (later King) Fuad I (r. 1917–1936) aroused British suspicions regarding a desire to strengthen his personal authority. When Fuad hinted that he wished to appoint individuals with apparent "nationalist" leanings to the cabinet, High Commissioner Wingate was caught in a quandary that only became worse by the end of the year. At issue was Fuad's suggestion that Saad Zaghlul be appointed Minister of Agriculture, with his close colleague 'Abd al'Aziz Fahmi (later one of the early political supporters of the Wafd) to be named to the Ministry of Religious Endowments.[7]

Opposition to Fuad's suggestion came, not yet from Wingate, who had high regard for Zaghlul, but from the Foreign Office itself. London wanted the security afforded by maintaining the two incumbents in these posts, mainly because of their open cooperation with British policy. The sudden political success of obviously privileged cabinet appointees such as Ahmad Ziwar Pasha, noted for his pro-British orientation, exacerbated the problems created by British preference for "known quantities."[8] Increasingly, anyone finding such high-handed Foreign Office favoritism unacceptable risked being labeled "nationalist," including the traditionally moderate Husayn Rushdi, cabinet head off and on during the 1914–1919 period, who continued to support Zaghlul as a candidate for a cabinet appointment.

Janice Terry's account of these moves in the last year of the war helps suggest why Saad Zaghlul would want to set out in new "nonconventional" directions. As events continued to unfold, he lost the tacit support of High Commissioner Reginald Wingate, who, now changing his view of Zaghlul's potential, seemed satisfied with compromises that were being imposed. In December 1917 he wrote to his Foreign Office superior Arthur Harding,

> Let us hope that, for the moment at any rate, we shall have no more advanced political programmes, though we must expect a very frank exposé of Nationalist aspirations when the war is over and . . . settlement has to be made on several pending questions.[9]

The Self-Appointed Wafd and Immediate Postwar
Maneuverings for and against Saad Zaghlul

Almost immediately after announcement of the Mudros Armistice in the fall of 1918, Saad Zagh-lul and a small group of supporters took upon themselves the task of forming a *wafd*, or "dele-gation," to present Egypt's postwar case in the upcoming peace talks in Paris. The events that followed help explain how, from this small, self-declared beginning, Zaghlul could attach an initially closely defined cause to suddenly emergent popular disturbances. These, as well as the shifting stakes in postwar political negotiations, would move at a pace unknown since the outset of the occupation regime.

As early as three months *before* the Armistice, discussions had apparently taken place between different individuals who contributed to the founding of the Wafd. Although several of these early Wafdists continued to play a role in Egypt's politics over the next decade, only one in the first round of negotiations with the British—Prince Umar Tusun—would attract poster artists' attention from the very outset and (over a three-year period, at least) serve as a useful but fre-quently controversial symbol of support for Saad Zaghlul.

Tusun reportedly met with Prime Minister Rushdi and several others before suggesting the delegation idea to Zaghlul sometime in October, 1918.[10] From that point, other prominent indi-viduals decided to lend their names to the nascent movement. The fact that *none* of these were represented in the earliest Wafd campaign posters—appearing only later when an "inner lead-ership" group under Zaghlul was formed—already suggests the beginnings of ambiguity. Given their recognized symbolic importance, who would be the presumed supporters of Zaghlul as head (*ra'is*) of the Wafd?

After initial confusion over whether Prince Tusun would head the proposed delegation or cede that place to Zaghlul, High Commissioner Wingate agreed to receive three self-assigned Wafdists—Zaghlul, 'Abd al-'Aziz Fahmi, and 'Ali Sharawi.[11] When Wingate learned that these delegates intended to ask for an end to the protectorate and full independence, he hesitated to take a position, pending instructions from London. Almost immediately, two other prominent Egyptian politicians, Prime Minister Rushdi and 'Adli Yakin, asked Wingate's approval *for them* to travel to London, a move made without conferring with Zaghlul. In any event, the Foreign Office proved unwilling to take up any part of the Egyptian question while preparations were underway for the main peace conference in Paris. Both Rushdi and Yakin would, however, figure among the symbolic supporters of Zaghlul in the coming Wafd poster campaign, this despite repeated tergiversations in their political maneuverings.

Janice Terry provides a detailed account of how different individuals reacted to the first signs of rivalry between potential leaders of the Wafd. By the time a Committee of Fourteen (all identified at the time as Zaghlul supporters) filed for passports to travel to Paris, an effort was undoubtedly underway to neutralize any challengers, in part by coopting persons who had had pre-1914 Watanist associations.[12] Prince Tusun was apparently one of these. His agreement not to form a separate del-egation probably induced some fence walkers to support the Committee of Fourteen. Yet it seems that the prince's position remained ambiguous, judging from the fact that he apparently would never hold an official position in the inner circles of the Wafd leadership. On the other hand, as we shall see, he was depicted in Wafd political campaign posters—at least up to a certain point—more frequently than most of the individuals who never wavered in their dedication to Zaghlul.

Meanwhile, Wafd supporters began what became their trademark as a popular political move-ment: they recruited followers in various towns and the countryside to carry the message of the Wafd's cause, outlined late in November 1918 in a twenty-six article program.[13] By this date, representatives of the Watan Party living in exile were busy preparing "memoirs" of their own for separate consideration in the upcoming Paris peace conference.[14] Knowledge of such actions by the exiled Watanist Muhammad Farid may have had the effect of inciting the Wafd group to move quickly to get their own program into British hands. In fact, Farid never actually aligned himself with Zaghlul's cause before his death in 1919, even though he is pictured as a supporter in many Wafd lithographs.

Wingate, who would soon be removed in favor of someone more willing to toe the Foreign Office's line, tended to support the Committee of Fourteen's bid to carry an Anglo-Egyptian negotiation plan to Europe. This bid was rejected in a telegram from London on November 27, 1918. The Foreign Office did not, however, rule out the possibility of receiving prime minister Rushdi and education minister 'Adli Yakin in London, not Paris—a move evidently gauged to split Egyptian nationalist loyalties.[15] Rushdi's and Yakin's rumored threat to resign over British maneuvers only delayed an impending confrontation. That London might be considering stronger measures to favor "the Ministers" (i.e., Rushdi and Yakin) over "the Extremists" (the Committee of Fourteen?) was hinted at in one high Foreign Office official's memo lamenting Wingate's unwillingness to see such a need. "The Ministers," he wrote,

> will not come to England unless the Extremists are allowed to come too. The Ministers . . . stress . . . the importance of conciliating the nationalist [*sic*] party. . . . There are objections to [another] course [that] may yet prove to be the best solution—to deport S. Z. and [fellow core Wafd member] Isma'il Sidqi from Egypt.[16]

A few months later, when that quite drastic course was actually adopted, and Zaghlul and three of his colleagues were arrested and deported aboard an Italian vessel to Malta on March 9, 1919, popular disturbances followed immediately, unleashing what later pronationalist historians labeled the "1919 Egyptian Revolution."

Arrest of Wafd Leaders and Popular Demonstrations

What began as student protests, most notably at al-Azhar, soon spread to crowds of workers and even lawyers supporting their "martyred" professional colleagues. As disturbances reached rural areas, armed British intervention resulted in a number of deaths. An unprecedented event occurred on March 16, 1919, when a core of women activists including Safiya Zaghlul herself and other well-to-do wives of Wafd organizers participated in a march through the streets of Cairo. The totally unparalleled event eventually earned a place of its own in contemporary Egyptian social and cultural history.[17] Protests reached their height in a mass demonstration involving students, workers, lawyers, and government employees. Although Janice Terry does not provide specific details, she is the first historian to describe use by Wafd supporters at this time of "political propaganda," including "posters and leaflets . . . distributed all over Egypt." Some pamphlets and even postcards included pictures of Saad and Safiya Zaghlul. "Soon," Terry suggests, "Zaghlul's features were familiar to all Egyptians."[18] Whether figure 2.1 actually dates from the period of disturbances that followed Zaghlul's deportation in March, 1919, it is definitely prototypical of the series of portraits of the Wafd leader that contributed, over the next few years, to the public's imagined perception of his persona: a serious and unswerving leader devoted to Egypt's drive for independence.[19]

It is equally difficult to determine whether other original lithographs depicting actual historic events during this initial period were done close to the time of their occurrence, or if posters like figures 2.2 and 2.3 were printed sometime later. If the latter is the case, both such examples of

2.1. His Excellency, the Head of the Egyptian Wafd, Saad Pasha Zaghlul. Courtesy of Special Collections, J. Willard Marriott Library, University of Utah.

2.2. (TOP) Egypt's Gentle Sex [Cries Out]: Forward!

2.3. (BOTTOM) Ceremony in Recognition of Martyrs Fallen in Cairo, Alexandria, Tanta, and al-Mansura
Both images courtesy of Lesley Lababidy.

anonymous propaganda graphics are perfect reflections of the "official" Wafd campaign posters that began to appear about two years later.

Figure 2.2 bears no identifiable provenance but definitely resembles near-contemporary photographs associated with the much-publicized Women's March in March 1919.[20] The lithographic version, of course, could have been done at any time after the event itself. Figure 2.3, on the other hand, contains internal evidence that it was done *before* political maneuvering gave the Wafd its distinct identity under the largely unquestioned leadership of Saad Zaghlul. The scene depicts a procession commemorating the deaths of twelve "martyrs [who fell] in Cairo, Alexandria, Tanta, and al-Mansura" during violent stages of demonstrations. Not only is Zaghlul's image *absent* here (something that almost never occurred during the coming period of Wafd propaganda), but the banner in the procession bears the name of the Watan Party![21]

Continuing deterioration of the situation led to acting Foreign Secretary Lord Curzon's move to isolate Reginald Wingate by sending "Special" High Commissioner General (later Field Marshal) Edmund Allenby to Cairo. Despite Curzon's expectation that he would follow a hard line dealing with the situation, Allenby began by meeting with Egyptian religious leaders, former government ministers, and several individuals directly associated with the Wafd. In return for their signatures on a document calling for a halt to demonstrations, Allenby took the first steps that would lead by the end of March to the freeing of the Wafdists held on Malta and, on April 11, the departure of most members of the original Egyptian Committee of Fourteen for Europe. From this point, factors intervene that may explain why Zaghlul would tend toward ever-more popular devices, including the possibility of "advertising" himself in graphic form as the irrefutable "head of the fatherland" (*ra'is al-watan*). Within the space of two years the term *ra'is*, and its feminine equivalent *ra'isa*, would be used widely by Wafd supporters (and thus by artists drawing the Wafd campaign posters) to refer to Zaghlul and his wife, Safiya.

Challenges to Zaghlul's Leadership within and beyond the Paris and London Delegation

There is considerable evidence, of course, of divisions between British policymakers over the evolving situation. On the Egyptian side, it is harder to find evidence of higher-level divisions in leadership goals. It may have been splits inside Wafdist ranks themselves, however, that best explain the use of propaganda posters to garner popular support for Zaghlul's *sole* leadership of the Wafd both in Europe and at home in Egypt.

The Ra'is himself was absent from Egypt until the early summer of 1920. Just as the Egyptian delegation was getting settled in Paris, Curzon, with Allenby's support, dispatched another high-level official to Egypt. Lord Alfred Milner was to

> inquire into the . . . late disorders in Egypt and to report on . . . the form of constitution which, *under the Protectorate*, will be best calculated to promote . . . the progressive development of self-governing institutions, and the protection of foreign interests.[22]

While Milner set to work to devise more fruitful directions for British policy in Egypt, Zaghlul was determined to influence the Milner Commission's work from afar. The Ra'is wanted Egyptians to boycott the commission's efforts and reject any compromise short of complete independence. Such intransigence seemed to yield results even before, and certainly after, Milner arrived in Egypt. Special High Commissioner Allenby was forced to use heavy-handed repressive measures to quell public demonstrations and violence that continued into the early months of 1920. The troubles included the attempted assassination of an unpopular prime minister suspected of working too closely with the British. Amid such continuing confusion and disillusioned by local advice that the mission should "see Zaghlul," Milner left Egypt in March 1920.[23] By June, only a few weeks after submitting his report to Curzon, Saad Zaghlul came from Paris to London to confer directly with Milner.

The Milner report became the basis for unexpected (by Curzon, at least) major changes in Britain's presence in Egypt, changes that were represented for many years in "The Four Reserved Points." In May 1920, Milner recommended a new "treaty" to replace the protectorate. The proposed agreement would give Egypt sovereignty over its internal governance as long as Britain (1) retained control over its existing military bases in Egypt; (2) continued to be responsible for defending Egypt from outside aggression; and (3) retained sole responsibility for capitulatory matters still applying to Egypt. The fourth "reserved point"—extended recognition of the Sudan as a (separate, essentially British controlled) Anglo-Egyptian condominium—not yet, but would soon become, a formal addendum.

Announcement of Milner's proposals sparked serious divisions among Wafd leaders and brought several key resignations in reaction to Zaghlul's handling of the situation from afar. It was soon clear that the Wafd central committee in Egypt would be unable to command full support for emerging lines of compromise. Not only extreme nationalists—including followers of the original Watan movement—rejected what Zaghlul seemed to accept. Some of his personal rivals (now including ʿAdli Yakin, his former collaborator by then seated as prime minister) inserted themselves between the British and supporters of Zaghlul. Janice Terry presents evidence that Prince Umar Tusun (who, as noted, later appeared a number of times in Wafd campaign posters) was aligning himself with *opponents* of the Milner-Zaghlul proposals. Milner found himself in a quandary: his superiors expected dispatch of "formal representatives of the Egyptian government" to undertake treaty negotiations—with or without Wafdist participation.[24]

The possibility that everything might fall through was increased by repeated outbreaks of violence on the part of extreme nationalists, as well as unsettling leadership changes in the Egyptian cabinet. It was obvious by the spring of 1921 that Zaghlul feared ʿAdli Yakin might succeed in co-opting core Wafdists. Thus, he left Paris early in April to return to Egypt to rally support for his claim to be the only truly popular leader speaking for all sectors of the Egyptian population, though perhaps not for all details of the Milner proposals.

Zaghlul's return on April 4, 1921, became the subject of one of the most colorful lithographs in the Marriott Library collection—one that includes the Raʾīs "escorted" by Prince Umar Tusun. The image, shown in figure 6.6, shows the two symbolic leaders passing before the equestrian statue of Ibrahim Pasha, icon of the family line whose dubious role was to head the eventually ill-fated Egyptian khedivate, sultanate, and then kingdom under indirect British control.

From this point the situation moved quickly, not in the direction the Wafdists would have preferred, but one that produced the unilateral British decision to end the protectorate along the lines Milner had favored from the outset. Paradoxically, Special High Commissioner Allenby was largely responsible both for precipitating the protectorate's end and saving Zaghlul from the onus that would have attached had it been the Raʾīs himself (and not the Yakin cabinet) who accepted the compromising terms handed down by the British in March 1922.

This chain of events led to even more suspicion between Zaghlul and Prime Minister ʿAdli Yakin. Yakin had denied any cabinet posts to loyal Wafdists but included Ismaʿil Sidqi, an early Wafd member who had fallen out with Zaghlul when the Wafd delegation was operating in Paris and London.

Moreover, the British decision came just as relations continued to deteriorate between the Wafd and the waning protectorate authority. Public unrest mounted daily, including several assassinations of British military personnel. These violent actions were not necessarily the result of Wafdist agitation, even if they did fit their desire to demonstrate intransigence. By December 1921, Allenby's patience had unraveled. He banned any further Wafd rallies and also laid the same groundwork to block Wafd mobilization efforts as had been tried unsuccessfully in 1919: preparations for Zaghlul's "reception and detention in one of H. M.'s possessions overseas."[25]

Unilateral End of the Protectorate and Zaghlul's Second Deportation

Zaghlul's continued intransigence, combined with heightened violence in Cairo's streets, convinced Allenby to use higher levels of police action. The Wafd leader was arrested on December 23. Zaghlul and several of his closest associates were transported by ship first to Aden and eventually to the Seychelles. Even while deportation procedures were still being carried out, Allenby threw down a challenge to both Foreign Secretary Curzon and Prime Minister Lloyd George to "get rid of the Protectorate. . . . [The] effect will be . . . that opinion in Egypt will be so mollified that the Egyptians will concede to your terms."[26]

Continuing the rapid unfoldment, Allenby threatened resignation unless the British government took his advice: end the protectorate under conditions defined by the Reserved Points. During March 1922, Egyptians learned that the protectorate had been ended and their sultan since 1917 would soon be recognized as King of Egypt. Apparently "no mention was made of the Wafdists or [their] leaders in exile . . . [thus highlighting] the British intention to undercut the party and to implement its [sic] own will on Egypt."[27]

Saad Zaghlul was freed a second time and returned to Egypt, this time under very changed circumstances and more than a year after the end of the protectorate. By the time he landed in Alexandria, a number of measures had already been taken to promulgate an Egyptian constitution in preparation for elections to Egypt's first National Assembly. Somewhat ironically, as he reentered the changed arena of Egyptian politics in September 1923, the Ra'îs apparently wanted to present himself as an image of moderation. He met with King Fuad and appeared publicly at Claridges Hotel in the company of his celebrated host Prince Umar Tusun.

Indeed, the time had become ripe—if Zaghlul aimed to attract voters to the Wafd cause in elections now just a few months away—to downplay the aura of extremism, violent demonstrations, and open denunciation of the British that had marked the two previous years. Thus, Wafd hopefuls behind the Ra'îs's candidacy looked in different directions to develop new propaganda methods. One of these directions took the form of popular and colorful posters produced by local artists experimenting with symbolic caricatured images that emphasized the benevolent role the Wafd was prepared to play. Egyptians of all strata of society would now be urged to follow Zaghlul's lead toward *al-istiqlâl al-tammâm,* complete independence.

We turn now to the main thematic questions pursued in the following chapters. To suggest answers, it is necessary to begin by exploring the wider field of political caricature art in the nineteenth and early twentieth centuries and to ask, when the first Wafd party campaign posters appeared, did they reflect an identifiable tradition of popular lithographic printing essentially redirected to serve local political needs? Or were they rather a transfer originating in graphic models common in Europe or other areas of the world, either within or beyond the borders of the Ottoman Empire?

Only a few historical references (most notably Janice Terry's seminal 1982 work) contain hints that, by the time of Egypt's first parliamentary electoral campaign, the Wafd movement had begun to use elementary pictorial graphics to garner popular support for its cause. Photographic collections from the period are important, of course, but if photos appeared as events unfolded (for example, in the Wafd newspaper *al-Balâgh*, the *Message*), what they tried to communicate—namely, immediate circumstances—would have been quite different from the early, original, hand-crafted public campaign posters.

No documentary evidence seems to exist that could tell us who determined the form and content of the popular graphics used by the Wafd in its earliest election campaign. We do know that a few small-scale printing establishments were operated by relatively unknown Egyptian lithographers well before 1919. As for Egyptian artists who had already made some name for themselves by printing politically motivated caricature art, only one name stands out for more than passing treatment: ʿAbd al-Hamid Zaki, publisher (from 1907 to 1908 in Cairo, then later from Bologna, Italy) of *al-Siyâsa al-muṣawwara*, or the *Cairo Punch*.[28]

The question that needs to be posed, then, is: since the moment seemed right for using graphics in Egypt's first popular election, what was the inspiration for the artists who drew the Wafd images? Obviously, a highly developed trade producing poster graphics had emerged elsewhere in the previous decades to distribute "popular art" for commercial, esthetic, or political purposes, particularly in Europe and North America. Did any of these precedents serve as models for the Egyptian lithographers whose work appears in the following chapters?

3

POLITICAL CARICATURE AND FOLK IMAGERY IN THE NINETEENTH CENTURY

Were European Prototypes Transferable to the Non–European World?

What were the precedents in the wider world of nineteenth-century caricature art, both in Europe and distant regions to the east, that might have been reflected somehow in the Wafd political posters in the early 1920s? It appears that two genres—one emphasizing satirical, often biting, images, the other "softer," tending toward folk imagery—are traceable through quite famous European prototypes that merit discussion before considering original lithographs done in non-European contexts.[1]

At least two well-known examples of Egyptian artists' adaptation of what we definitely can call "European inspired" satirical caricature emerged in the unique political context of *pre-1914 Egypt*. Both are focal topics in the next chapter. The closer one looks at these two cases, however, the more it appears that peculiar circumstances governed the way any local Egyptian adaptations of European models may have taken place. This is also true in terms of the potential viewing audience to which they were directed. What may have appeared to obviously exceptional Egyptian artists in the pre-1914 period as inviting prototypes did not, it seems, fit well in the postwar environment. On the other hand, a much simpler, nonsatiric caricatural approach that used folk imagery and simple symbolism offered more chances of success in the relatively unsophisticated sociopolitical Egyptian environment of the time.

At first glance, there seems to have been no prior existence in Egypt of graphics, satirical or not, using the simple caricatural imagery that appeared in Wafd 1922–1923 campaign posters. Further investigation, however, suggests that little-known precedents—all untraceable to European models—did exist as part of a local commercial market for mainly nonpolitical popular posters printed as lithographs in the late Ottoman period. These may well have lent themselves to repurposing for political propaganda when the need arose. Within this process one frequently encounters the name of a particular lithographer, ʿAbd al-Hamid Zaki.

Zaki's career in the first decade of the twentieth-century definitely linked him to the conscious practice of political satire along the general lines of European caricature art.[2] Then, as a prime mover in adapting an already existing genre of folk imagery to the emerging need for simple political graphics, he began to experiment with quite different caricatural styles. This peculiarly Egyptian amalgam did not "borrow" from European models. Neither, however, did it simply continue an elementary commercial art form that had begun to use folk imagery for popular audiences living in various regions of the declining Ottoman Empire.

Early European Lithographic Methods and Uses

What were some of the European prototypes that created a medium for advanced artistic expression through lithography as well as a growing tradition of political caricature art during the nineteenth century? It is well known that lithographic techniques developed in this period lent themselves to uses ranging from the simplest graphics to very sophisticated works of art.[3] Within this broad field emerged a whole world of caricature art—a world that naturally invited political satire and symbolism as well as more "comforting" depictions of folk imagery.

After its first development in Germany at the end of the eighteenth century by Alois Senefelder, lithography spread to all sectors of the printing industry. On the one hand, highly skilled printers were contracted to serve many well-known artists both in Europe and North America, from such greats as Francisco de Goya and Eugène Delacroix early in the new century to Edgar Degas and James McNeill Whistler just prior to the twentieth century. On the other hand, it was clear that the technique could be used to produce much less sophisticated art.

As a vehicle for printing elaborate caricature art, a high point was reached when French newspapers published (to take but one case) the famous illustrations of Honoré Daumier (1808–1879). Daumier became known for sophisticated scenarios that followed main issues of the day. He produced political and satirical caricatures, epitomized by his *Legislative Belly* (*Le ventre législatif*), depicting (in amusingly exaggerated drawings) twenty-seven identifiable members of France's legislative assembly in 1834.[4] At the same time, he did a variety of humorous, only indirectly political caricatures of everyday life, many including the self-contented and well-fed Monsieur Prud'homme.[5]

Although discussion here will be limited to consideration of only one famous illustrated journal, *Punch*, or the *London Charivari* (founded in 1841 by Henry Mayhew and Ebenezer Landells), several well-known satirical magazines, not only those in France and England (*Le charivari* and *Punch*, of course, but also *Il Papagallo* and *Fanfulla* in Italy), provided "classic" models for many coming generations of European and American caricaturists. The degree to which such European prototypes may have lent inspiration to later nineteenth-century artists as far away as India, Japan, and the Middle East is an ongoing subject of research.[6] For the moment, the major point for emphasis is the fact that lithography made it possible to distribute all manner of printed images to all levels of society, first in Europe and North America and eventually across the globe.

Many volumes have been written describing the use of lithography for mass production of a wide variety of posters for public viewing and private collecting.[7] Posters were also used throughout the nineteenth century as a medium to publicize political causes and candidacies or, of course, to oppose or ridicule. Beyond political purposes, posters served as advertisements for social and cultural events and propaganda in times of crisis—military conflicts and revolutionary upheavals in the early twentieth century are obvious cases. Poster artists in the latter instances drew heavily on shocking images and symbolism to rivet viewers' attention on urgent needs for unity and support.[8] Such symbolism often tended toward exaggerated representation, making it difficult to distinguish between caricatured images of real persons and disturbing fantasy.

Poster art in support of particular causes or individuals in both normal and "emergency" political settings also relied extensively on symbolism to communicate ideas on the subconscious level. In cases where a majority of viewers might not be literate, similar methods, some involving popular folk imagery, played to simpler levels of imagination. Contrasting examples of such symbolism from different geographical regions and historical settings (but from approximately the same period as the posters we will be examining) suggest how widely such artistic choices could vary from one sociocultural context to another.[9]

A Search for Precedents in Nineteenth-Century European Caricature Art: Simple Folk Imagery vs. Open Satire

A first step toward establishing such contrasts inevitably means returning to the rapidly developing mid-nineteenth-century European lithograph "industry." There, one finds useful examples of what will be viewed in this book as folk imagery—combined with symbolism and some elements of political caricature—beginning as early as the 1830s in the French *Images d'Épinal* series. The sheer number and diversity of *Images d'Épinal* printed in, or associated with, the eastern French town of Épinal precludes discussion of the full gamut of colorful images.[10] Our interest here lies in the popular genre that such prints represent, plus the fact that founder Jean-Charles Pellerin's themes often contained symbolic representations of idealized "patriotic" scenes imbued with simple elements of folk imagery. Such scenes were mainly drawn from well-known events in French history rather than controversial contemporary politics. This generalization would not hold, however, when France and Europe plunged into the 1914–1918 war. During those years, many *Images* artists turned their attention to propagandistic, strongly anti-German themes.[11]

In the pre-1914 period, common Épinal lithographs often portrayed folk or fairy tale personages (Cinderella, or the folk tradition of the Prodigal Son, for example) and other popular images attractive to both children and adults. There were also portrayals of famous but distant moments in French political history, especially from both Napoleonic periods. Unlike strongly political caricatures that would spread to other areas of the world based on famous European prototypes, but somewhat like the caricatures found in selected Ottoman imperial and Egyptian lithographs, any satire in Épinal images was meant to convey light amusement, never shocked reaction.

Apparently neither of the two examples of Épinal images reproduced here bore the names of the artists when they were originally printed. Charles Lacour (figure 3.1) and Jean-Charles Pellerin himself (figure 3.2) were identified later when these drawings were published in a collection of Épinal prints in 1912.[12] Both share essential characteristics of folk imagery since they were drawn with the more or less conscious intent of eliciting pleasant associations among the common people who viewed them.

Figure 3.1 conveys the onlookers' jubilation watching two trains passing a nearby village. Although unremarkable, the image is typical and "comforting" and includes small houses in a pastoral setting, wafting chimney smoke, and even a quaint windmill. The folk imagery style here makes it appropriate to show both male and female onlookers (in addition to an obviously excited dog), some dressed in modest styles common to rural areas, others sporting more sophisticated clothing, including a man with a top hat. One uniformed figure, possibly a military officer or soldier, rounds off the representative nature of the scenario.

Figure 3.2, one of four scenes by Pellerin depicting the creation of the world, is simple to the point of naïveté—obviously intended. Apart from the anthropomorphic image of the Creator, which follows careful stylistic norms appropriate to the subject, other sections of the scene are treated without undue concern for detail or accuracy. This applies to the imagined contours

LE CHEMIN DE FER.

Image dessinée probablement par Lacour (dimensions du bois 29 × 56).

3.1. The Railroad. Image in the public domain.

of the horizon, miscellaneous scattered vegetation, and especially Pellerin's drawings of a few selected animals, all (except one idyllically grazing sheep) gazing at their Creator. In numerous illustrations like these, artists contributing to the *Images d'Épinal* generally made every scene as simple as possible, communicating a certain comfort in folk imagery. Of course, figures 3.1 and 3.2 both include some symbolism, but it is symbolism of the simplest kind.

So characteristic was the folk imagery reflected in prints produced during the press's long life that, for the French, the term Épinal image "a pris au fil du temps un sens figuré, qui désigne une vision emphatique, traditionnelle et naïve, qui ne montre que le bon côté des choses"; or, "The term Épinal image has, over time, taken on a figurative meaning, one that suggests an emphatic vision both traditional and naïve, which shows only the good side of things."[13]

Although it is too early in the discussion to begin examination of the quite different world of lithographic production leading to the main topic—popular graphics in pre- and post-1918 Egypt—figure 3.3 suggests how one can approach certain early-twentieth-century Egyptian lithographs in the same "Épinalist" spirit, that of an "emphatic vision, both traditional and naïve, [showing] . . . only the good side of things."

This example of popular caricature art was the product of what we will later identify as simple "keepsake art" printed by local Egyptian lithographers around the turn of the century.[14] It is only one illustration suggesting possible comparisons with the "traditional and naïve" style that characterized the work of *Images d'Épinal* artists. First, figure 3.3 depicts, without need for further commentary, the Judeo-Christian-Islamic tradition of the Prophet Noah and the Ark. The simplicity (but one should add immediately, endearing attraction) of the drawing and particularly the animals crowded aboard, comes close to communicating the "good side of things" that one might see in typical Épinal images.

Thus, it seems that, when elements of folk imagery are involved, it may be easier to cross breaches between different cultures than is the case when more complicated subjects dominate—particularly political issues or satirical nuances.

Collection de la maison Pellerin.

3.2. The Creation of the World. Image in the public domain.

Many other examples of popular lithographs produced either for the periodical press or as individual decorative prints for commercial distribution in Europe or North America could be reviewed here. But attention needs to be given to a second developing theme before turning to lithographic artists on other continents: caricatured images in openly political contexts, often conveying satire and/or humor.

Perhaps for English-speakers the most famous illustrated periodical employing cartoon images combining three familiar elements—caricature, satire, and humor—for political aims was the British illustrated weekly, *Punch, or the London Charivari.*[15] The relevance of a few selected examples of illustrations from late-nineteenth-century *Punch* issues here will become apparent when its prototypical mode of satire was transferred to other totally different locations in time and global culture.

In contrast to the popular, often "everyday" subjects in the *Images d'Épinal, Punch*'s graphic scenarios were usually political. When symbols were used to convey satirical messages, those in *Punch* were most often aimed at a well-informed, if not to say quite sophisticated, audience. In short, the complexity of *Punch* artists' depiction of their subjects—unlike Épinal images—generally ruled out use of folk imagery. A few samplings from *Punch*'s own 1900 publication, *An Evening with Punch*, illustrate ways in which its artists combined caricature, political satire, and—when the situation was appropriate, as it often was—open humor.[16]

No social or political grouping, and no well-known contemporary public figure was immune from *Punch* caricaturists' roving imagination. For example, an illustration from February 23, 1889, (part of a series by Harry Furniss labeled *Essence of Parliament,* this one entitled *Meeting of the Gods*) combined caricature portraits of identifiable members of parliament (including Gladstone wielding a primitive bludgeon, another M. P. playing a harp, others simply asleep) with imaginary images of Roman gods. The most grotesque reclining deity is a smiling *male* Venus (also probably an identifiable M. P. of the time) overseeing the generally chaotic scene.[17]

3.3. Noah's Ark. Courtesy of Special Collections, J. Willard Marriott Library, University of Utah.

Proof that no high-ranking individual was immune from sardonic treatment by *Punch* appeared in the August 3, 1889 drawing *Visiting Grandmamma*, by Sir John Tenniel.[18] Figure 3.4 shows Queen Victoria telling a diminutive but adult Kaiser Wilhelm (son of Victoria's eldest daughter) who holds a toy shovel next to a sand castle replete with toy soldiers: "Now, Willie dear, you've plenty of soldiers at home; look at these pretty ships, I'm sure you'll be pleased with them!" This is a reference to the impending (and ultimately openly rival) expansion of military naval forces that would be pursued by both countries by the end of the century.

One last, chronologically earlier, example of *Punch*'s satirical approach to the maneuverings of Britain's political elite implied criticism of Her Majesty's Government's increasing involvement in the 1870s in the affairs of the Egyptian Khedivate. A December 1875 graphic captioned "Mosé in Egitto!!!," ("Moses in Egypt!") in Italian, also by John Tenniel, was a satirical vision of Prime Minister Benjamin Disraeli's controversial purchase for the British government of a majority percentage of shares in the Suez Canal.[19] The drawing includes a turbaned Disraeli holding a giant Suez Canal key, "The Key of India," while exchanging glances with the Sphinx. Disraeli's gesture (index finger held to the side of the nose, suggesting a shared secret) elicits a smile from the Sphinx.

This might logically seem to be the place to introduce possible transfers, eventually to the Ottoman Middle Eastern region, of at least some elements of satiric political caricature found in European journals such as *Punch* or the French *Le Charivari*. Rather sweeping suggestions of transfers of satirical journalism, including *some* satirical graphics, do appear in Elif Elmas's recent study, "Teodor Kassab's Adaption of the Ottoman Shadow Theatre Karagöz."[20] Closer examination, however, suggests that scholars are not completely clear concerning the content of the surprisingly numerous journals cited. In the case of Kassab's main and quite well-known

[*By Sir John Tenniel.*]

VISITING GRANDMAMMA.

GRANDMA' VICTORIA. "NOW, WILLIE DEAR, YOU 'VE PLENTY OF *SOLDIERS* AT HOME; LOOK AT THESE PRETTY *SHIPS*,—I 'M SURE YOU 'LL BE PLEASED WITH *THEM!*"

[*August 3, 1889.—Vol. 97, p. 55.*]

3.4. Visiting Grandmamma. Image in the public domain.

3.5. The Key to India. Image in the public domain.

publication after 1873, *Hayal* (*Imagination*), it seems that most of the graphics were both closely tied to Hacivat and Karagöz, Ottoman shadow-play figures, and caricature models "imported" from Europe. Kassab had his Turkish equivalents of Punch and Judy play out scenarios that reflected the artist-playwright's own personal cultural ideas concerning the role of theatrical arts within the sultan's domains. His repeated critical and satirical treatment focused on a field that was, in Elmas's words, "more than other art forms . . . a symbol of social change in the Ottoman Empire."[21] It is probable, therefore, that Kassab's readers would have been mainly from the higher ranks of society, invited to consider his satirical drawings as reflections of "transformations [via European influence] in language, literature, education, fashion . . . and entertainment culture" in contemporary elite Ottoman circles.[22]

The fact that *Hayal* remained so closely tied to Kassab's specific concern for theater arts leaves us looking elsewhere in the Ottoman Empire for pre–World War I graphics that suggest products of mainly local artistic approaches though perhaps initially inspired by European caricatural tradition.[23] That the twain were far from meeting is graphically most evident through comparisons of the most likely field for political propaganda, if not satire, and certainly not humor: caricatures appearing in the Ottoman Empire just before or during World War I.

Although one can find politically motivated lithographs dating before the war, almost all examples appear to have been "officially sponsored." Most were illustrations connected with the ruling sultan's authority and/or the main religious tradition of the empire. By definition, therefore, caricatural representations having pre-1914 Ottoman provenances did not contain satirical elements and tended to repeat stereotypic themes. It appears, however, that—when official sultanic or military emphasis was not the core concern—some did contain elements reflecting simple folk imagery.

Comparison of examples of European and Ottoman propaganda graphics suggests that by the time of World War I two quite distinct sources of inspiration influenced propaganda illustrations originating in the Islamic zone that stretched from Turkey to Asian regions. There would be hardly any borrowing from European models visible in surviving Ottoman lithographs. This was in contrast to late-nineteenth-century caricature art originating, most importantly, in India and even farther east in Asia. In the main, models that appeared in the Ottoman Empire were *sui generis*. This stands out clearly when one compares European caricatures targeting the sultan's empire and "locally initiated" graphics distributed in the Ottoman region during approximately the same period.

European and Ottoman Wartime Caricature Art: European Satire vs. Ottoman "Sobriety"

Generally speaking, and excepting of course the many grim posters that both the Allied and Central Powers produced during World War I, *Punch* and other European satirical publications repeatedly poked fun at their wartime enemies, including the Ottoman Sultanate.

The most familiar target of Allied propaganda, before and after 1914, serious and satirical, was of course Kaiser Wilhelm II. But with the coming of the war, the figure of the Ottoman Sultan began to rise in importance. Examples of European propaganda graphics referring specifically to the Middle Eastern zone during World War I are rather rare, at least by comparison to posters focused on the Western or the Russian fronts.[24] However, for a limited number of examples, one can turn to the contemporary *Mr. Punch's History of the Great War*, which contains caricatures representing the Turk in obviously negative but characteristically satirical terms.[25]

Two examples of wartime symbolic images of the Turk were by *Punch* artist Sir John Bernard Partridge (1861–1945). The first (not reproduced here) was entitled *William O' the Wisp*.[26]

ALSO RAN

WILHELM: "Are you luring them on, like me?"
MEHMED: "I'm afraid I am!"

3.6. Also Ran. Image in the public domain.

It shows an obviously bewildered Sultan Mehmed V regretting "the hour when Allah bound me tight to [Kaiser] William's chariot wheels!" The second Partridge caricature, entitled *Also Ran*, (figure 3.6) can be tentatively dated from internal evidence near the end of 1916.[27]

Also Ran shows Kaiser Wilhelm and a harried Turkish sultan, both running in different directions following signposts leading to the Ancre River (the November 1916 battle site marking German defeat in the last stage of the Battle of the Somme) on one hand, and to Mesopotamia (marking the major 1916 Allied advance against the Turks in Iraq) on the other. In the caption, Wilhelm asks the sultan, "Are you luring them on, like me?"[28]

Although *Punch*'s caricatures of the Turkish-German alliance were generally infused with sardonic humor, this was not necessarily the approach of its Gallic counterpart *Le Charivari*. In fact, its view of the Turco-German enemy tended to be just that: a picture of dangerous and hateful opponents. This vision appears in the November 22, 1916 issue of *Le Charivari* in which dancing German and Turkish soldiers gleefully spread flaming petroleum. The same graphic depicts cruel German and Turkish military discipline involving officers whipping half-clothed soldiers and, in the Turkish case, lashing the bare feet of recruits chained to a bench.[29]

One might have expected that such anti-Ottoman images would have elicited comparable hostile, possibly satirical, reactions from Turkish propagandists. But Ottoman "officially sponsored" posters followed quite different artistic modes. First, there were few, if any options for private printing establishments to experiment, even if they wanted to, with satirical caricature

3.7. The Young Ottoman Movement, 1876. Image in the public domain.

graphics even remotely similar to what was produced by Europeans west or east of the Rhine. In fact, when reactions came—in the form of posters extolling the presumed military power and combined secular and religious legitimacy of the sultanate—these drew little inspiration at all from Western models.

Although politically motivated images supporting the legitimacy of the sultan's realm in this period used expected stereotypic symbolism, they eventually came to include—unexpectedly—some features that could be qualified as folk imagery. But, conforming to strictly defined cultural norms for "popular art," they contained no humor or ironic satire. This applies equally to lithographs that were obviously symbolic representations of the personal authority of the sultan and to graphics that, although political in nature, can be identified as popular commercial prints experimenting with different but still culturally circumscribed subject matter. In stages, this combination of propagandistic stereotypes and popular folk imagery would contribute to the way pre-World War I caricature art from a broader Ottoman context was transmitted to the focal arena of post-1918 Egyptian political graphics.

Symbolism and Folk Imagery in Ottoman "Official" Lithography

A number of examples of "official" Ottoman lithography can be found for the period starting with the Young Turk constitutional restoration of 1908 into the first years of World War I. A quite different body of illustrations from about the same period—lithographs representing various well-known buildings in Istanbul, views of the capital, or countryside vistas and main provincial

3.8. Proclamation de la Constitution—le 24 Juillet 1908. Courtesy of Professor Recep Bozetemur, Middle East Technical University, Ankara, Turkey.

cities—have also survived in significant numbers. While these do not aid our search for vestiges of political caricature and sociocultural symbolism, one finds some interesting examples that suggest how recognizable cultural symbolism, especially graphics dealing with widely accepted and popular Islamic religious subjects, could and *did* come to encompass political themes.

Early twentieth-century Ottoman posters displaying clear propagandistic themes were usually connected with the 1876 or 1908 proconstitutionalist coups or Turkish military campaigns as early as the defense of Tripolitania against Italy in 1911–1912 and the Balkan Wars of 1912–1913.[30] Then, of course, World War I itself became the paramount object of "official" propaganda. What turned out to be abortive political developments in the same broad chronological period provided a different arena for nascent Ottoman caricature art. Figures 3.7 and 3.8 offer examples of typical propaganda posters symbolizing the Ottoman constitutionalist movement's desire to "liberate" all the sultan's subjects, first under 'Abd al-Hamid II (r. 1876–1909) and then under Sultan Mehmed V (r. 1909–1918).[31] Such posters began in 1876, quickly faded, and then reemerged after 1908.

The two examples here are particularly relevant for our purposes because they definitely seem to be harbingers of the almost entirely secular artistic style combining symbolism and folk imagery found in the Egyptian Wafd posters some ten years later.

Although Figure 3.7 is not dated, it was probably done soon after supporters of the Young Ottoman movement proclaimed, in 1876, the constitutionalist coup that placed 'Abd al-Hamid II on the throne. Because 'Abd al-Hamid suspended the 1876 Constitution (and most political freedoms) two years later, it is understandable that the naïve enthusiasm contained in this lithograph was also "suspended" graphically during the long interim between this drawing and the scene in figure 3.8.

Figure 3.8 marks the 1908 restoration of the 1876 constitution by the Committee of Union and Progress, the Young Turks. Striking similarities between the two posters justify considering

| Political Caricature and Folk Imagery in the Nineteenth Century

them representative of a single genre, particularly when contrasted with very different types of Ottoman propaganda that began to appear once the euphoria of 1908 was again dampened by authoritarian measures.

Figure 3.7 bears a signature that suggests it was drawn by an artist from the Greek minority community. It openly emphasizes the 1876 "Midhat" Constitution's promise of equality for minority subjects of the Empire. The symbolism here is quite elementary. In the foreground are the historic leaders of the Young Ottoman movement. Each, including Midhat Pasha, is identified by name with apparently quite accurate depictions of their facial features. The leaders aid the hopeful, idealized female figure representing, not Greece itself (forcibly separated from the sultanate in the 1830s), but all members of the Greek minority community, rising from long years of unequal status within the empire. Liberation is obviously symbolized by the breaking of her chains.

The mixed composition of the supportive crowd of flag-bearing onlookers reinforces the enthusiasm for "Liberty, Equality, and Fraternity" inscribed in Turkish and Greek on the banner carried aloft by an angelic figure. Equal respect for minority Christian and majority Muslim popular identities (and perhaps also a meeting between traditional conservative and Western-oriented effendi values) is represented by differences in individual clothing and—ever important at *all* social levels—headdress style. One should note, however, that onlookers here, in contrast to the depiction of the 1908 constitutional restoration (figure 3.8), are all male.

Scholars of Ottoman (and then post-1920 Turkish) iconography, especially Palmira Brummett, take careful note of early-twentieth-century caricatured representations of women in different graphics produced after 1908. At least three prototypic examples reproduced in a 1997 article by Brummett offer idealized symbols of late Ottoman womanhood that can be compared with the images in figure 3.8. One in particular, a 1909 caricature from the journal *Lak Lak*, shows a traditionally clad and obviously idealized Turkish woman bound at the feet by ball and chain. The artist who did the 1909 drawing, however, did not place the scene in a recognizable Ottoman cultural context. The woman symbolizing the plight of the Empire is surrounded by diminutive figures representing the European powers.[32] In such a case, it is difficult to suggest any further intended symbolism tying the idealized feminine figure ("the Empire") to specifically Ottoman sociocultural values of any sort.

Despite certain differences in detail, figures 3.7 and 3.8 share feelings of euphoria associated with political "liberation." Moreover, both use simple folk images that call to mind the elementary techniques found in typical Épinal lithographs. Identifying such techniques in these first-selected, non-European examples could help in the search for prototypes that might have inspired the creators of the Wafd posters in a totally different historical but similar cultural context.

Certainly the panoramic physical setting in figure 3.7—an imaginary view of Istanbul from the shoreline looking toward the (arbitrarily placed) Topkapi heights—"frees" the artist from having to represent the actual physical reality of the setting. In the foreground is an ostensibly European-style building with highly simplified depictions of curious viewers in its windows. The viewers overlook what the artist's imagination has transformed into a totally empty stretch of land and the unfolding momentous events, perhaps the graphic equivalent of poetic license.

The scene in figure 3.8 is also obviously meant to provide reassurance of the benevolent (firm, but now once again constitutionally limited) authority of the sultan. ('Abd al-Hamid II reigned until 1909.) This is done by including with his portrait a whole gamut of symbols of power. The symbols involve two levels of symbolic headdress: a military tarbush *and* a ceremonial turban. All fall under the rays of the sultan's highly respected calligraphic *tughra* or imperial monogram, in addition to standard symbols of military preparedness. The entire scene is framed by inscriptions welcoming restoration of the constitution in Arabic, Greek, and French. The scrolled banner in the center repeats the "Liberty, Equality and Fraternity" pledge and adds additional symbols of minority support for the pledge in Hebrew and Cyrillic scripts.

While clothing variations do not allow easy identification of different ethnic groups here, figure 3.8 contains a symbolic message that was innovative for its time: almost all figures on the right side of the banner-bearing throng are women, and all are clothed in simple, generic Western dresses. At the same time all the women are pictured *without* head coverings. Although less immediately apparent, two men in a group dominated by tarbush wearers (no turbans present) stand out for an absence of any head covering at all—a very rare occurrence anywhere in the Islamic world at the time.

In sum, it appears that at this early period of the Young Turk government symbols of progressive leadership and signs of some changing social values were in vogue among caricaturists supporting the new regime—at least until the pressure of circumstances moved the Istanbul regime in a more authoritarian direction just before World War I. Such symbols would recede, however, rather quickly.

Reflections of Rising Military Pressure

After 1909, the person of 'Abd al-Hamid's successor, Mehmet V, figured prominently in almost all graphics supporting the legitimacy of the Ottoman constitutional monarchy. His portrait, whether bust size or full-figure standing, is almost always surrounded by symbolic images. In addition to formal frontal portraits in which resplendent military regalia emphasizes his position as imperial commander, "secondary" symbols of wartime preparedness soon became more and more apparent.

Figure 3.9, for example, shows Mehmed V in military attire surrounded by a number of earlier sultans in traditional robes and turbans. Beneath the regularly aligned portraits are various accoutrements of war (cannon balls, swords, and trumpets) and two military scenes: naval squadrons steaming forward, and marching columns preceded by mounted troops.[33]

When Ottoman posters of the period depict actual military conflicts, the sultan sometimes appears as an observer, as in figure 3.10, commemorating the battleship *Hamidieh* sinking Greek and Serbian transport ships off the Albanian coast during the First Balkan War.[34] This graphic (done sometime after 1911) was one of several printed by the Egyptian lithographer and founder of the *Cairo Punch*, 'Abd al-Hamid Zaki.

A second poster, also by Zaki (figure 3.11 "H.I.M. The Sultan Mohame V [*sic*] Saluting His Troops Going to the Battlefield"), was in all likelihood near the same date as the *Hamidieh* naval scene.[35]

Two other military propaganda posters, one dated 1326 AH (1908 CE) picturing an "Ottoman Dreadnought" at sea, and a second done seven years later, commemorating the 1915 World War I battle on the Gallipoli Peninsula, were printed without marginal captions indicating their provenance. Neither of these contains the symbolic images of the sultan that appeared in so many contemporary images.

Commercially Produced Complements to Official Images: Introduction of Popular Islamic Themes

Although posters emphasizing Ottoman military preparedness before, and certainly after 1914, have their own inherent interest, a broader, culturally based framework supporting the ruling

3.9. Sultan Mehmet V. Image in the public domain.

legitimacy of the sultanate was also expressed graphically, usually through symbolic associations with Islam. Surviving examples suggest, more than obvious military propaganda, at least distant connections with later graphics associated with post–World War I Egyptian popular art and political caricatures.

It is well known that, especially during and after the sultanate of ʿAbd al-Hamid II, an attraction to pan-Islamism became part of the political program of the empire in its last stages.[36] Of course, there would have been "official" propagandistic channels—mainly the subsidized periodical press—to express the regime's espousal of pan-Islamism. The appearance of a variety of commercially produced lithographs representing popular religious themes with only minimal captioning, however, may have been intended to complement formal governmental propaganda efforts via newspapers. Although we do not know particulars concerning their distribution, it is likely that some printers counted on such posters becoming popular enough to attract "everyday" buyers— most likely from kiosks that received limited packets of locally printed materials. In 1948, the British Museum acquired an important collection of posters that answer this description. They may help us trace the changing content and graphic style of such privately published propaganda posters.[37]

Quite different sources of inspiration appear in posters popularizing imperial leadership through intentionally secular parliamentary images on one hand and imperial association with traditional Islamic religious practices on the other. Examples in the British Museum's 1948

3.10. (TOP) The Battleship *Hamidieh* . . . off the Coast of Albania
3.11. (BOTTOM) H.I.M. the Sultan Mohame [*sic*] V Saluting His Troops Going to the Battlefield
Both images courtesy of Nehal El-Naggar.

3.12. Al-Madina el Menawwarah: The Great Mosque of the Prophet Mohammed. © The Trustees of the British Museum.

collection in the latter ("traditional Islamic") category clearly outnumber images acknowledging the secular identity of the restored Ottoman Parliament. One of two involving secular themes, *The Opening of the Ottoman Parliament*, shows a solemn group seated on benches before an anonymous speaker.[38] The second is entitled *H.I.M. the Sultan Abdul-Hamid II Opening the New Parliament*, thus dating it between 1908 and 1909.[39]

The same collection also includes quite different religiously oriented lithographs, probably for a more general audience. The only indirect political messages in these are conveyed by the juxtaposition of symbols of religious tradition alongside the imperial Ottoman flag. In one such poster, accompanying captions and occasional inclusion of a minimal per-print price suggest that *Al-Madina el Menawwarah* (*The Illuminated City—Medina*, Islam's second-most holy city) and others of the same type were printed in or near 1910 for commercial distribution.[40]

Al-Madina el Menawwarah, like the scenes of Ottoman military maneuvers just mentioned, were done by 'Abd al-Hamid Zaki's *Cairo Punch* press, raising again the question of how and why the editor of the originally highly satirical and visibly European-inspired publication turned his attention to such popular (and modestly commercial) graphic subjects.

Lack of Graphic Equivalents between Europe and the "East"

It seems clear, therefore, that there was a lack of even indirect equivalents in popular Ottoman propagandistic graphics, when compared with Western propaganda images before and during

World War I. Particularly absent in Ottoman posters are any elements of satire whatsoever. What, then, could have been the source of inspiration that "transferred" at least some elements of pre-1914 styles in Ottoman graphics to a quite different Egyptian context soon after the empire was dismantled?

To answer this question, we must first have some idea of the potential audience that might have existed in Egypt at the time these Ottoman graphics were produced. What sort of climate was developing in Egypt that might have provided a window for adapting locally produced caricature art to serve what would turn out to be a totally new Egyptian political cause? Chapter 4 explores at least two quite well-known earlier vehicles of Egyptian caricature art—in particular 'Abd al-Hamid Zaki's *Cairo Punch*—before that press itself became involved, for whatever reasons, in producing prewar Ottoman propaganda. Did any of these earlier Egyptian experiences with caricature art inspire the unexpected directions taken by graphic artists who later decided to support the Wafd's postwar nationalist cause?[41]

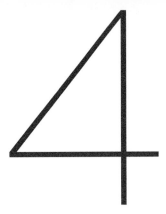

PUNCH SATIRICAL PROTOTYPES "EXPORTED" TO CULTURALLY RESTRICTED AUDIENCES BEYOND EUROPE

The Awadh Punch *in India, Egypt's* Abou Naddara, *and* al–Siyâsa al–muṣawwara *(the* Cairo Punch)

The limited but well-known precedents of political caricature in Egypt did not inspire the simple graphics that supported the country's first truly popular nationalist movement after World War I. Rather, it appears that a redirection of folk imagery—considerably simplified popular images from local artists—was intended to attract supporters to the Wafd.

Before describing the somewhat segmented trail that led to commercial distribution in Egypt of popular political posters, several questions need to be addressed. Anyone interested in mid- to later-twentieth-century Egyptian journalism frequently encounters mention of the importance of caricature art, including the rather sophisticated satirical political cartoons published from the mid-1920s forward.[1] What can be gained by reopening the question of where Egypt's early and increasingly important role in the genre began? The discussion here will offer an informed guess concerning sources behind the somewhat obscure and elementary Egyptian caricature art that will be discussed in chapter 5.

I suggest a "missing link" between two periods of political caricature art in Egypt that have already received considerable scholarly attention. It does appear that significant graphic material was overlooked, or perhaps deemed of lesser importance. Instead, scholars have focused on better-known—arguably elitist—pre-1914 caricatures and, as the diverse literature shows, the even more famous satirical representations from the interwar period and later. To what extent were such "missing-link" precedents reflective of the local cultural milieu in which they appeared? Were they in any way "copies" inspired by someone else's experimentation with caricature art?

To take just one example here of "second channel" precedents, figure 4.1 bears interesting signs of "Egyptianization" in an anonymous artist's perception of immediate post–World War I conditions governing the ceremonial obligations of Sultan Mehmet VI, the last Ottoman Sultan (r. 1918–1922).[2] In terms of subject matter, the scene is simple enough. The sultan's cortege carrying him to Friday prayers passes before a military review and a small gathering of respectful

4.1. Mounted Procession . . . of Sultan Mehmed VI. Courtesy of Lesley Lababidy.

private onlookers. The caricatural inspiration in the lithograph, however, suggests that the artist was an Egyptian "stretching his imagination" to create a setting that—if meant to represent the Topkapi Palace grounds—lent Egyptian features to an Istanbul he had never visited.[3]

Some elements of style here do resemble prewar Ottoman forerunners, such as figures 3.7 and 3.8. Comparison with the poster commemorating the martyrdom of Egyptian political demonstrators between 1919 and 1921 in figure 2.3 (apparently in the still-lingering name of the Watan Party), however, suggests that both were done by the same artist at approximately the same date—given their marginal captions and representation of private onlookers. Both graphics reveal a tendency for the artist to "invent" folk imagery only beginning to appear in earlier "official" Ottoman political caricature art. This question will gain in importance if the little known nonpolitical, nonsatirical graphics introduced in the next chapter are, as they do appear to be, truly authentic products of an Egyptian cultural milieu. One thing should become increasingly clear: such lithographs, as well as the campaign posters produced for the Wafd's post-1918 electoral campaign, would be very different from the much better-known product of Egyptian artists (arguably inspired by European prototypes) discussed later in this chapter. The problem, then, will be to fit little-known or little-recognized "missing links" into what appears to be renewed scholarly debate over the origins of early Egyptian caricature art, particularly in caricatures containing humor or satire.

Setting the Scene for Satirical Caricature in Egypt: Pre–1914 Precedents

Professor Marilyn Booth's 2013 article "What's in a Name: Branding *Punch* in Cairo," questions Afaf Lutfi al-Sayyid Marsot's assumption, made more than thirty years earlier, that "the graphic cartoon was not used [in Egypt] in the period between 1880 and 1920."[4] If we place the term "caricature" as a near synonym alongside the more familiar but semantically restrictive word "cartoon," it may help place Professor Marsot's statement into a broader historical context. In fact, with only one important exception—the presumed necessity of *satire* as part of cartoon/caricature art—her description of the genre could apply well to all the pre– and post–World War I graphics, whether European or non-Western. In addition to her conviction that "[s]atire is one of the basic elements of the cartoon," Marsot states,

> [T]he function of any cartoon [from here forward assume the alternative phrase "*cartoon or caricature*"] is to influence the spectator for or against something, either by presenting it as a figure worthy of sympathy, or by distorting it into a figure of ridicule. . . . [Thus] . . . a cartoon is a form of satire which aims at creating or influencing public opinion through social and political criticism.

She also suggests,

> [A] cartoon [or caricature] purports to reveal the "reality" behind a public figure or a situation, but a reality which is in fact a distortion designed by the artist for the . . . purpose of influencing the spectator.[5]

This definition certainly applies to the satirical images extracted from *Punch* in our earlier chapter on the one hand, and even to "comforting" folk imagery in drawings from the *Images d'Épinal* press on the other. Professor Marsot's emphasis on satire as a necessary component of cartoon or caricature art, however, precludes including the late Ottoman and post–World War I Egyptian graphics that are of primary interest to us under her general definition.

The 1971 "Cartoon in Egypt" article did, however, set the tone for several later studies examining the two most important landmarks of *pre-1920* caricature art produced by Egyptian-run presses, both of which *did* have satire at their core. Both, although at first published in Egypt itself, were later obliged to reach subscribers (in Egypt, but also in other regions, including Europe) by alternative means after their presses were transferred abroad. The most famous and long-running, *Abu naḍḍâra zarqâ'* (the Man with the Blue Spectacles, hereafter *Abou Naddara*) featured articles and satirical political caricatures by James Sanua. Sanua continues, up to the present, to be among the few nineteenth- to mid-twentieth-century Egyptian caricaturists who receive very widespread popular and scholarly attention in Egyptian and foreign publications.[6]

The second early twentieth-century Egyptian caricatural publication, previously mentioned, is the lesser-known *al-Siyâsa al-muṣawwara*, the *Cairo Punch*, introduced between 1907 and 1908 by ʿAbd al-Hamid Zaki.

We can probably assume that both Sanua's and Zaki's precedent-setting illustrated publications, certainly more so than the very wide-ranging graphics selected by Palmira Brummett from the Ottoman press between 1908 and 1911, would have been at least familiar to the limited number of small-scale lithographers in Egypt well before World War I.[7] It appears, however, that the strongly satirical political content of such earlier works that were actually (or at least initially) printed in Egypt did *not* provide inspiration for the much more elementary caricature art produced by local publishers during the "missing-link" period from the immediate prewar years into the early 1920s. On the other hand, evidence exists suggesting that the quite different path that ʿAbd al-Hamid Zaki followed as an illustrator in the interim years between 1908 and World War I *did* share many characteristics with other lesser-known contemporary Egyptian lithographers who may also have been inspired by his work after 1908. This alternative path led to the production of a variety of posters in a totally different style, eventually including those that supported the Wafd after 1918.

In fact, as noted earlier, from about 1908 (while apparently still publishing *some* satirical graphics in the name of the only recently launched *Cairo Punch*), Zaki had already begun shifting away from the sophisticated satirical models that characterized his better-known, if brief, earlier years as an illustrator. In order to understand how and when that shift occurred (creating a "second channel" after 1918), a survey of the early content of the *Cairo Punch* and pre-1908 satirical graphics is necessary.

Sophisticated Symbolism and Folk Imagery Reflected in India and Egypt before 1908

Considerable time could be spent trying to explain the apparent "disconnect" between the sophisticated graphic world of earlier quite well-known publications such as *Abou Naddara* or the original *Cairo Punch* and the elementary popular Egyptian poster art printed just before and after World War I. Short of this, an obviously abbreviated account of both illustrated journals will help explain the artistically unique styles that surface so prominently in the JWM/Utah and LL/Cairo Wafd poster collections.

Here, we survey the work of three well-known satirical caricaturists: one (among many) in colonial India and two in Egypt.[8] All three used caricatures similar to those that could conceivably have appealed just as well to sophisticated readers of European satirical publications of the same time period. Moreover, their images were also like those in Palmira Brummett's study of political satire in Istanbul gazettes published during the brief period of restored constitutional government between 1908 and 1911.

Fortunately for this synoptic review, considerable new source material and scholarly analysis for two of these original artists was published in 2013 in *Asian Punches: A Transcultural Affair*.[9] Equally recent contributions by researchers in India suggest that, initially, it was in India that the illustrated satirical journalism first established in Europe received widest recognition before the turn of the twentieth century. Some of the features of satirical caricature in Indian publications such as the *Awadh Punch* may have been carried over, consciously or not, to the Cairo journal that later, also borrowed the name of the famous London periodical. But by the time the *Cairo Punch* chose to participate in the post-1918 Wafd poster campaign, it had already begun "Egyptianizing" its graphics. By that date, in fact, the caricature artists who joined their illustrations to those of the *Cairo Punch* during the Wafd's first political campaign adopted and adapted local features that were very different from the "flashiness" of the few illustrators (including Zaki himself) who had experimented with European-style political satire and symbolism over the previous decade. This style not only merits comparison with prototypes pioneered by the English *Punch*, it also clearly confirms Professor Marsot's earlier noted definition of satire.

Sophisticated Satirical Prototypes before 1914: The *Awadh Punch* in Northern India

The political caricature journals reviewed here and in the rest of the chapter contained symbolism and at least some folk imagery that was very different from the "comforting" scenes in *Images d'Épinal*. Most importantly, among the limited examples one finds of political caricature art in non-Western regions in the late nineteenth century, many consciously emphasized strong satirical political agendas—especially those from different regions of India under British rule.

In this respect, publications such as the *Awadh Punch* can be compared both to European prototypes and to 'Abd al-Hamid Zaki's early caricatural campaign when he founded *al-Siyâsa al-muṣawwara/Cairo Punch* in 1907. On the other hand, neither the *Awadh Punch* in India nor the early issues of the *Cairo Punch* suggest linkages with the sober, scarcely ever satirical (if perhaps whimsical) tones that dominated Egyptian artists' use of folk imagery in popular illustrations that combined simple cultural values with very modest political causes before, and particularly after, World War I.

The strong political messages artists sought to convey in the *Awadh Punch*, for example, were so obvious that they rendered secondary any folk imagery that might be present. Such imagery might recall daily life in provincial settings, but a certain degree of viewer sophistication would have been necessary to decipher the (not at all comforting) messages intended, as with European satirical prototypes.

In the case of *Awadh Punch* founder, Sajjad Husain, family origins alone may have impelled him toward a journalistic and artistic career that emphasized both sophisticated and politically sensitive issues. His interests eventually encompassed Britain's position in his native Northwest Provinces, colonial India as a whole, and broader global issues connected with colonialism.

Husain was the son of an administrator in the British provincial government who rose to the rank of civil judge under the Nizam of Hyderabad. His uncle held an even more prestigious post as Chief Justice of Hyderabad.[10] Husain's educational background already pointed to both local elite status and a high level of consciousness concerning social, cultural, and political institutions in the Lucknow district. By the age of twelve he was enrolled in the prestigious Canning College of Lucknow. According to Mushirul Hasan's extensive monograph on the *Awadh Punch*, Husain shared Canning College experiences with a number of equally privileged students who would take part in the journal's publication over the years. Some of these were illustrators, while others supplied poetic captions for the *Awadh Punch*'s highly diversified graphics.

Only a short time passed between Husain's graduation in 1874 and his purchase of a lithographic press. In 1877, he founded the illustrated Urdu-language *Awadh Punch*. A brief summary here of the *Awadh Punch*'s choice of subjects and graphic techniques provides what we need to compare its political caricatures with those that appeared about the same time in Egypt's *Abou Naddara* and, after 1907, the first years of the *Cairo Punch*.

Articles and illustrations in the *Awadh Punch* tended toward penetrating satire but without the humorous undercurrents so characteristic of its eponymous forerunner in England. From its earliest years, it grew ever closer to the Indian Congress Movement, founded in 1885. Thus, one could expect it to be at least moderately critical of the Raj administration. But in fact, there was hardly a local or international topic covered by the *Awadh Punch* that did not include some form of caricatured and, most often, clearly uncomplimentary image of easily identifiable British colonial representatives.

Figure 4.2, one of Husain's earliest caricatures, was apparently inspired by an earlier illustration that appeared in *Fun* magazine depicting a "motherly" image of India with the Prince of Wales on her lap during his 1875 visit to India.[11] Here, the *Awadh Punch* (June 15, 1880) imagined a similar satirical scene to mark the arrival of the newly appointed Viceroy, the Earl of Lytton, in 1876. Various toys are strewn about the "child" viceroy and the motherly figure of Hind. These, including an elephant turned on its back, may represent "amusements" available for Lord Lytton's distraction. Symbolism attaching to the small, baked figures impaled on Mother India's arrow suggests a more subtle message: Indian mothers commonly offered such tidbits to their children to calm them or reward good behavior. In contrast to the abstract symbolism in Ottoman posters using female figures with little relation to the "everyday" life of the empire (figure 3.7 in particular), Hind in this picture seems to call to mind familiar family scenes. Hence, she could be said to reflect a stylized folk image of Mother India.[12]

والسبرائے جدید

4.2. Governor-General Lord Lytton arrives in India in 1876. Image in the public domain.

4.3. Yaqûb Khan (Defeated in the Anglo-Afghan War, 1878–1880). Image in the public domain.

Egyptian caricaturists eventual use of Mother Egypt images, although quite different from the image of Mother India here, will be seen in later selected examples to share one feature: evocation of symbols familiar to common folk observers.

In addition to simply satirical images, illustrated editorials in the *Awadh Punch* frequently took up serious issues that lent themselves to more unpleasant symbolism. Figure 4.3, published on December 9, 1879, refers to recent British successes in the Second Anglo-Afghan War (1878–1880). Top military officer Sir Frederick Roberts offers comfort and assurance to the imaginary feminine image of Kabul, following defeat of the bewildered Amir Muhammad Yaqûb Khan. The caption refers to a poem by the Urdu- and Persian-language poet Ghalib in which a departing lover expresses remorse leaving the "pleasant paths and sweet companionship" of his mistress—a somewhat daring editorial quip to say the least!

Other, openly grim subjects invited similar sardonic reflections. In figure 4.4 published on January 27, 1880, Maharaja Ranbir Singh of Kashmir shows Viceroy Lord Lytton—accompanied by a rather unintimidating imperial lion—a petition assuring the Raj of his people's faith in the maharaja's good government. The maharaja, however, shields from Lytton's view a female figure representing the helpless Kashmiri population threatened by famine and death himself. In Urdu, Lytton remarks, "Quite so, I have seen this, and it is all very well, but what is that behind you?"

One could choose a number of examples of caricatures that depict quite different politically sensitive causes. Many picture the grim material conditions suffered by disadvantaged sectors of the local population. Others focus on particular administrative or legislative issues, such as rising Hindu *and* Muslim opposition to a proposed Age of Consent bill in 1891 to protect young Indian girls from family forced marriages. But the *Awadh Punch* also directed its criticism well beyond

شیر ـ "چڑائے سے بہو ہٹا ہے ؞ قاتل ہیں لوگا ؞ وفادارون کے خون کا دلہ کیا وہ تہاسے کچرا کاٹھ

4.4. The Maharajah of Kashmir and Viceroy Lord Lytton. Image in the public domain.

local colonial concerns in drawings revealing its broad satirical point of view. These include, for example, a later (July 19, 1906) caricature of the Sultan of Turkey dressed in a turkey-feather costume blowing "empty bubbles" labeled Aqaba (the key port linked to the Anglo-Ottoman "Taba Affair" described in chapter 1). It is captioned "The Impending Calamity."[13] Husain's caustic eye, coming so close to events in Istanbul that led to the 1908 Young Turk constitutional coup, begs the question of parallels between the *Awadh Punch*'s caricatural style by this date and similar (definitely European-inspired) images traced by Palmira Brummett in her monograph, *Image and Imperialism in the Ottoman Revolutionary Press, 1908–1911*.[14]

Before considering the earliest examples of illustrated political satire to appear in Egypt itself before World War I, it is interesting to note that the *Awadh Punch* occasionally published satirical drawings specifically criticizing Britain's position in Egypt. An example of how *Punch* itself approached the Egyptian Question came in chapter 3 and in a caricature mocking Prime Minister Disraeli's controversial purchase, with government funds, of a majority of Suez Canal company shares (figure 3.5). The *Awadh Punch* published its own satirical opinion of England's position in Egypt with similar notes of symbolism, beginning with a September 1891 drawing of John Bull astride an Egyptian donkey. The Egyptian situation itself, as well as the *Awadh Punch* view of it, grew in complexity when, fourteen years later, the advent of World War I changed British policy from occupation to imposed protectorate. The interventionist move is symbolized in an October 12, 1915, graphic depicting a human figure with multiple arms and heads standing on stacks of documents surmounted by a donkey's head (again representing Egypt?) pronouncing the slogan, "Placing the curse of one's [Egypt's] poverty on the other's head."[15]

Sophisticated Egyptian Satirical Prototypes before 1908: *Abou Naddara* and the *Cairo Punch*

Comparison of such caricatures in *Awadh Punch* with images in two of Egypt's best-known satirical publications in about the same time period confirms that the three journals shared several similarities. Certainly, Professor Afaf Marsot's summation of James Sanua's *Abou Naddara* experimentation with political cartoons, "really a foreign import which Sanua . . . introduced into Egypt, but [lacked enough time] . . . to grow roots *in the native soil*," is not far from the mark.[16] Despite obvious differences in content, influences stemming from London's *Punch* or France's *Le Charivari* appeared in both Egyptian journals (as they clearly did in *Awadh Punch*) under a similar imported veneer.

Here, a caveat exists that should apply to any discussion of possible links between examples of political caricatures published in India and the earliest comparable experiments in Egypt. First, the individuals who launched the first publications with lithographic illustrations in both the Indian and Egyptian cases shared some key attributes with artists who contributed to European periodicals such as *Punch*. All sought, rather aggressively, to make a particular mark for their names and reputations when they entered the publishing arena. Simple folk imagery and its effects on "popular" appreciation of the types of themes presented was not foremost in such publicists' minds.

Of the two Egyptian publications considered here, James Sanua's contribution to Egypt's late-nineteenth-century political and intellectual history is clearly better known than that of the editor of the *Cairo Punch*. This is largely because of the different historical conditions surrounding each journal's publication and what we know of their founders' very distinct careers. In this regard, a number of scholars have traced the rather tumultuous record of how Sanua's writings and caricatures expanded from what must have started as a limited audience in Egypt and abroad.[17]

Sanua's extensive work is of particular interest here for its high level of sophistication, comparable to images in *Awadh Punch* and the original *Cairo Punch*. This stands in contrast to the popular commercial lithographs that eventually found expression, however ephemeral, in Egyptian caricature art—not necessarily in association with the Wafd party—just before World War I.

Given the unique circumstances of Sanua's childhood and early adult years, he seemed from the outset destined for a life centering on art and *belles lettres*. Indeed, before his career as a playwright and satirical publicist, one could not have seen him as an activist, first in the local political setting of Egypt and, eventually, in a much wider, internationally recognized, anticolonial context. When this did happen, his soon-to-be notorious writings and drawings would be inspired by elements that were even more removed from the "simple" reflections of folk imagery expressed in *Awadh Punch*.

From a very early age, Sanua, born to an Italian Jewish father and an Egyptian mother, was exposed to a milieu that combined traditional Egyptian "court" circles and growing European influences among local elites. His father served in the household of direct descendants of Muhammad Ali. By the time Muhammad Ali's grandson 'Abbas I became Governor of Egypt (r. 1848–1854), high-level patronage made it possible for Sanua to complete his education in Livorno, Italy, where he studied arts and literature. In the mid-1850s, social and educational privileges enabled him to begin a teaching career in Egypt in the newly established *muhandiskhane*, which resembled a polytechnic high school. This came just as Said (r. 1854–1863) replaced 'Abbas, marking the early stages of Egypt's opening to different forms of European influence.

James Sanua must have judged that such signs of change had already created a receptive environment for new forms of Egyptian social and cultural expression. As it was, his first contribution to the anticipated trends—founding his own theatrical group—met with mixed reaction. His debut as a playwright received initial encouragement from Khedive Isma'il in the late 1860s. This was just as Egypt drew world attention at the sumptuous opening of the Suez Canal and the inauguration, among other "showpieces," of Cairo's first opera house. But, almost immediately controversy over antipolygamy implications in his play *al-Darratayn* (*The Two Co-Wives*) may have led to Isma'il's decision to close Sanua's fledgling theatre.[18] From this point almost everything he undertook would earn him a reputation for radical opposition to the khedivate and biting satire of the Egyptian ruling elite. These attributes were readily apparent in the first issue of *Abou Naddara* in March 1878 and accelerated as internal and international complications continued to buffet the khedivate.

This first phase of Sanua's controversial publishing career inside Egypt itself was quite short-lived. Isma'il reacted almost immediately to stem the overt criticism in *Abou Naddara's* first fifteen issues. Sanua's press was closed down and he was forced into exile in France in 1879. As soon as Sanua found French sponsors, however, he returned to what became a long career of illustrated satirical journalism aimed from afar at the regime that had first supported then abruptly rejected his artistic talents.

Dr. Eliane Ettmüller's extensive research on *Abou Naddara* considers whether Sanua's artistic work, with all its unique and interesting features, offered a model for later artists who used caricatured graphics for nationalist political aims in Egypt. In a 2013 article, Ettmüller studies the thirty issues of illustrated installments (August 7, 1878–March 13, 1879) entitled *Riḥla abû naḍḍâra min miṣr al-qâhira illa bârîs* (*Abou Naddara's Journey from Cairo to Paris*).[19] Ettmüller points out that Sanua presented Abou Naddara, the protagonist of the *Riḥla* vignettes, in a way that was evidently inspired by the well-known figure of Mr. Punch. This primary figure "play acted" Punch-like roles and rather obviously represented the editor/artist himself.

It is an understatement to say that the content of the *Riḥla* and later issues of *Abou Naddara* published from abroad show Sanua driven by a personal urge to denounce corruption within the ruling circles of Egypt. To this, he would add a strong anti-British bias that eventually widened to include colonial targets in other regions by the turn of the century. Indeed, although publication of *Abou Naddara* became both a personal mission and commercial venture aimed in large part at an audience far removed from local events in Egypt, its message may have caused as many reverberations in cosmopolitan international circles as in Egypt itself.[20] In fact, looking beyond the 1878–1879 *Riḥla* caricatures to the extensive corpus of satirical graphics that Sanua published in Paris over the next few decades only strengthens Marsot's suggestion that the style he introduced "was really a foreign import [lacking] roots in the native soil."[21]

From the outset, Sanua pursued a form of caricature art that used grim sarcasm, more than simple satire, to produce strong emotional reaction. Several illustrations Ettmüller chose from the *Riḥla* help make this point. One, in the October 8, 1878, issue, shows a peasant using physical force to beat down tax collectors serving the khedive.[22] The officials are revived only after receiving embarrassing aid from their subordinate, a humble commoner. This only adds to their confusion since (as one learns from the accompanying text) they move quickly to keep the fact of receiving help from a simple aide secret at all costs.

Another example of Sanua's use of sardonic caricature to illustrate grim aspects of Egyptian life appears in his sketch of an imagined meeting of a secret society organized by *Abou Naddara* (for the "conspirator" *Abou Naddara*, read Sanua himself).[23] The drawing evokes a scene in a theater, with curtains and backdrop. Society members confer solemnly without visible concern for the painted background behind them. The background scene shows a caricature of *shakyh al-ḥâra* (head of the city quarter), representing the khedive himself, calmly smoking a pipe while gazing at the decapitated heads of his enemies displayed on pickets.

هذا اخر عددس جرايد أبي نظاره رزقا خادم الحريه المصريه التي استمر نشرها مده ثلاثة سـنوات وحررها يطلب النجاح الى النظارات المصريه

أبوالعلم عزيز مصر يطارد البومه واولادها اللي درجانين جراب الد ويريد ا بنصوه ا ببسم

Le Prince Sauveur chasse le hibou de la Favorita et ses enfants que contemplent avec joie la destruction de l'Egypte   Nº 30.

4.5. Le Prince Sauveur, or 'Abû al-Ḥilm, "the Patient Man." Reproduced by permission from Eliane Ettmüller.

If one compares graphic sketches such as these with caricatures that appeared at about the same period in *Awadh Punch*, two common features are evident. First, choice of pictorial scenes invariably involves politically intense issues thrust to the immediate forefront with little room to doubt what the artist wanted to convey. Second, both use exaggeration to shock the viewer's eye at first sight. This is of course the opposite of symbolism based on commonplace figures and eliminates any room for folk imagery. In both cases, grimness is often reflected in the artist's chosen subject matter. The observation is borne out in figure 4.5, one of the last *Abou Naddara* caricatures Sanua printed (in the early months of 1879).[24]

Here Sanua uses the figure of Abû al-Ḥilm, "The Patient Man," or "The Savior Prince" in the French portion of the caption, as the idealized and "highly esteemed *ally* of the nation," who brandishes a staff to beat down figurative representatives of the khedivate who apply grotesque and pitiless methods to control the governed.

Given these characteristics of Sanua's career as a caricaturist, and adding the fact of physical separation between Paris in the late 1870s and day-to-day life in distant Egypt, I believe that the likelihood that *Abou Naddara* inspired later publishers of caricatured lithographs in Egypt itself was essentially marginal.

It is well known that his career as a publicist/cartoonist in exile did continue over a number of years, indeed quite successfully, until his death in 1912. Multiple examples of topics he developed over the years suggest that Sanua sought not only to draw attention to the dual cause of opposing the ineffective and corrupt khedival government of Egypt and England's lingering occupation regime but also to topics that took him through a wide labyrinth of contemporary international affairs. This helped gain him a reputation among rather select intellectual circles in Europe and even brought honorific awards from foreign sovereigns, including the Shah of Persia and the Ottoman Sultan, whose capital he visited and from which he wrote highly complimentary dispatches. Again, such highly publicized actions suggest that he was as much interested in gaining the attention of cosmopolitan European readers as in inciting serious vibrations in Egyptian politics.

No doubt Sanua's work does invite speculation as to how subjects that were peculiarly Egyptian lent themselves to future caricaturists' choices of topics, as well as methods of representation and distribution to specifically Egyptian viewers. When such choices involved the need to incorporate symbolism and folk imagery easily understood by unsophisticated Egyptians, however, the genre that Sanua developed must have been considered far beyond the world vision of the majority of the population.

Before and After: The *Cairo Punch*'s Satirical Political Caricatures before 'Abd al-Hamid Zaki's Unexpected Transition

On first sight, 'Abd al-Hamid Zaki was a somewhat different type of Egyptian artist who might have followed the satirical path opened by Sanua. Yet Zaki eventually chose to weave less-sophisticated elements into the work of his *Cairo Punch* press. The result, which came in the second phase of a long career, offered simply drawn, modest caricature art in which Egyptian viewers could recognize themselves and their everyday cultural values.

Zaki's caricatural drawings initially appeared in his openly satirical and highly political *Cairo Punch* between 1907 and 1908. At that point, his work seems to have tried, by various means, to address a very different sociocultural and political audience.[25] This shift provides a rather logical explanation of how, following a series of interesting if little-known examples in the *Cairo Punch* after 1908, the styles of symbolism and folk imagery that characteristized the Wafd's first campaign posters appeared in Egypt just before World War I.

As noted, during an interim from 1908 to about 1916 (after having moved his press from Cairo to Bologna, Italy), Zaki apparently gained wide experience producing lithographs *unconnected* with Egyptian subjects per se. Surviving examples from those years come much closer to the graphics adopted by the Wafd than the more famous drawings that established his reputation when he launched the *Cairo Punch* in 1907. At the same time, material documentable in *Cairo Punch* publications *after* 1908, especially the JWM/Utah and LL/Cairo lithographs, helps pursue questions raised, but left pending, in Marilyn Booth's 2013 article "What's in a Name?" and in her subsequent correspondence with the author.[26]

Biographical information for Zaki is unfortunately rather limited. His own statement in the second issue of the *Cairo Punch* and a somewhat vague reference in a widely recognized early history of the Arabic-language press suggest training as an army officer.[27] Dr. Booth's description of Zaki as "a white collar worker with some education" begs elaboration.[28] Her second suggestion—that Zaki planned from the outset to express strong condemnation of Britain's growing colonial role—is reflected in multiple declarations from early issues.[29]

From the outset, the *Cairo Punch* editor informed his readers that, as "The Only Oriental ... Political Colored Caricatured Journal," his paper would use his drawing skills to illustrate articles written by his poet friend Hafiz Ibrahim. Each four-page issue that followed over the next year contained strongly anticolonial articles accompanied by a large (double page) lithographic print. A number of these appear, with extensive commentary, in Marilyn Booth's "What's in a Name?"[30] What follows are only summary remarks to connect several questions of interest covered in

Professor Booth's article. Because the concern here is to introduce factors that may have affected caricature art in Egypt *after* the earliest issues of the *Cairo Punch*, the following commentary provides only partial impressions that should be completed by referring to Booth's more detailed research.

Comparison of early illustrations in the *Cairo Punch* with both earlier and contemporary drawings by James Sanua suggests that both caricaturists aimed primarily at a well-informed (and therefore somewhat limited) audience opposed to England's occupation of Egypt. Already in his second issue, it was apparent that Zaki would not hesitate to use strongly critical caricatures—whether as symbols or as exaggerated depictions of known personalities—to denounce British and Western imperialism generally.

In his untitled satirical drawing from December 27, 1907, Egypt counts as one of three nonsettler British colonies—along with Sudan and India—pictured symbolically as a group of distasteful creatures: scorpion, cockroach, and viper, respectively.[31] British settler colonies Australia and Transvaal also appear as less foreboding zoomorphs (butterfly and bat). The dominant central figure is a bigger-than-life, cigar-smoking John Bull himself, sporting "angel" wings. Also in the scene are smaller caricatures of other European nations, all in military regalia, looking on as John Bull proclaims (in English, French, and Arabic), "I am the one whose command orders all the seas and lands; I am the one who has put in servitude all those in the western lands and the eastern lands." On a hillside overlooking the scene a relatively "innocuous" figure representing the emergent Asian colonial power of Japan makes friendly signs across the field to a flute-playing, almost bucolic caricature of an American colonial revolutionary. The caption suggests that American success in repulsing British colonialism saved them from being included "amongst the subjugated and ludicrous insects."

This lithograph and others that followed in 1908 contained many of the same elements of sardonic humor that had appeared earlier in *Awadh Punch*. Most contain direct or indirect criticism of the British occupation in Egypt, set within satirical and heavily symbolic scenes filled with exaggerated figures.[32] Needless to say, whenever it was a question of drawing a figure representing Britain, the result was always uncomplimentary!

A different type of incisive satire appeared in the *Cairo Punch* April 17, 1908, issue under the title *Fi sabil al-taqaddum* (*On the Path of Progress*).[33] Zaki's subject here underlines Egypt's dilemma as it responded to growing pressures to "Europeanize," bringing social, cultural, and political strains. The scene draws attention, in an obviously satirical way, to questions of gender relations in some (certainly not all) effendi circles. In an Egyptian street scene, five onlookers clad in the overdone (bordering on flashy) attire of young effendis, plus a uniformed police officer, gawk at a dapper young gentleman strolling with a bejeweled and (transparently) veiled young woman. The woman's richly adorned traditional robes scarcely camouflage what the artist intended: everything about the couple suggests that they wish to be objects of attention and are dressed to assure that aim. A second woman (equally veiled, as Booth suggests, "in name only") at the window of a carriage considers accepting a proffered bouquet from another dandy. The only traditionally clad figures in the drawing—an elderly, turbaned shaykh who appears disconcerted and two peasants conversing in the background—are essentially out of place, not part of the "modern" city scene. The Arabic caption completes the satirical message:

> Truly Egypt in this era lacks nothing that is found in the civilized nations. Just look at her youths with their flirting, her young women with their transgressions.... This [*sic*, probably "Thus"] the apparatus of civilization is made complete and the conditions of progress amongst men and women are amply supplied.[34]

It is interesting to note that a similar, even more exaggerated example satirizing superficial adoption of Western social modes appeared in the *Awadh Punch* more than fifteen years earlier (July 3, 1890), entitled *European Civilization in Africa*.[35] Hussein's drawing there was of a steam locomotive driven into a station stop by two Africans in somewhat odd Western garb (one barefoot) who stare at a group of male and female African travelers. The latter sport totally outlandish clothing. The cigar-smoking men wear top hats, checked short trousers over leggings and spats, again without shoes, while two women with garish hairstyles and clinging dresses appear to be patting a full-size, tame male lion—the typical caricatured symbol of Britain.

By producing pictures that (like many in Sanua's *Abou Naddara*) mocked the presumed benevolence of the occupying authority, Zaki's early *Cairo Punch* deliberately set out to attract attention from well-informed, sophisticated readers opposed to Britain's position in Egypt. Of course, such readers would need to have enough knowledge of prevailing circumstances to be able to gauge the intended message. Saad Zaghlul, minister of education from 1906–1908, for example, *could* have been typical of the Egyptian educated class able to read between the lines (if indeed they read them) of articles and illustrations in these early issues of the *Cairo Punch*. This would not have been the case, of course, for the great majority of Egyptians.

Like Sanua, Zaki was initially visibly swayed by the temptation to attract foreign, perhaps as much as Egyptian, viewers of his sarcastic criticism of Britain's occupation of Egypt. A bare six months after his first issue, he took pride in announcing that the London journal the *Review of Reviews*, as well as the *New York Times*, had reproduced examples of his drawings, albeit noticeably altered.[36]

Two of the most frequently cited caricatures from the immediate pre–World War I issues of the *Cairo Punch* came just about the time Zaki moved his press to Italy in 1908. Indeed, these two alone reveal enough bitterness to perhaps explain the timing of the relocation of his printing operations, whether voluntary or forced. Both use satire and symbolism to revisit the perennial question of concern to all Egyptians and the international community as a whole: how long would the British stay in Egypt, and what methods would they use to impose their will?

The Modern Civilization of Europe: France in Morocco and England in Egypt (figure 4.6), with the Arabic subcaption *Remembrance of Denshawai*, plus a second print (not reproduced here) entitled *The English Councilors*, are part of a collection of original *Cairo Punch* lithographs held by the United States Library of Congress.[37] Both present bitter commentary on British actions that predated or (in the case of *The English Councilors*) were near contemporary with Zaki's efforts to denounce the Occupation regime. Figure 4.6, printed in the summer of 1908, "commemorated" conclusion of the 1904 Entente Cordiale between Britain and France, according to which both parties recognized one another's privileged positions in Egypt and Morocco.[38] British and French military officers congratulate each other over champagne for their respective "successes" in the two areas. Both foreground (a corpse and two mounds of skulls) and background (burning buildings in Morocco and gallows behind the British officer in Egypt, representing the notorious executions after the 1906 Denshawai incident) complete the grim satire.

The English Councilors, less grim than *Modern Civilization*, still carries a strong satirical message. It was probably printed during 1908, the year Zaki moved to Bologna. It can probably be considered within this date range because its central figure, Sir Eldon Gorst, served as British Agent and Consul General in Egypt after 1907 until his death in 1911. Gorst is pictured in the early years of his appointment lounging on a reclining chair—seltzer syphon, a glass, and a bell at hand—holding the strings that control seven puppets representing Egyptian ministers. There is a picture of the Pyramids on the wall, with an angry Sphinx straining to enter the room through the picture frame. Less obvious, but very important in setting the background for later

4.6. The Modern Civilization of Europe. Courtesy of Nehal El-Naggar.

developments, especially Zaki's decision to support the Wafd, the caricatured drawings of the puppet ministers are based on the actual facial features of each. The top center minister puppet is a rendering of the future founder of the Wafd, Saad Zaghlul himself, then serving (1906–1910, without yet showing open signs of opposition to the British occupation regime) as minister of education.

Modern Civilization, with its picture of the appalling executions after Denshawai, definitely roused British ire against the *Cairo Punch*'s artistic defiance of what occupation authorities hoped would be reasonable standards of self-censure. Booth's quote from Zaki's July 17, 1908, *We and the Foreigners* response to the scandal that *Modern Civilization* created leaves little doubt that his publishing days on Egyptian soil were likely to be limited.

> We thought we would remind the occupying nation of the deeds it has done here, so we portrayed Dinshaway—and the English justice entailed in it is clear for all to see. Next to it we showed Casablanca—and the French justice there is clear.

Zaki concluded with even stronger language.

> Would the English like . . . the French to occupy their country? If so, then we will be content with this wrong and tyranny. Otherwise, though, we hate the English and . . . will despise them from our hearts as long as they occupy our country.[39]

It is certainly of more than passing interest that near this juncture Zaki moved his press to Italy. The *Cairo Punch* not only began issuing "special editions" (such as *Dhikr Dinshawai*) for paid-up subscribers but also added signs of small-scale commercial initiatives to its columns. Beginning in about March 1908, a regular announcement appeared offering, for a reasonable price, personalized "mementos"—"images in oils with colors"—based on photographs sent in by private customers. Offers to print packets of original illustrations for "merchants who desire them for marketing" were also printed at this time.[40] Was this a sign that, under changing conditions affecting his ability to keep the *Cairo Punch* press operating, Zaki was tempted to shift his graphic emphasis from political satire to more mundane subjects? Marilyn Booth's view of this juncture suggests that the potential commercial use of the *Cairo Punch*'s press—and therefore the nature of the caricature art it would publish over the next few years—represents a "disconnect" from Zaki's original goals as a caricature artist.[41]

Two little-known library collections of Zaki's lithographic work leading into the first years of World War I (especially materials in the British Museum) offer evidence that the early images from the *Cairo Punch* and satirical "special issue" graphics such as *The English Councilors* are not the most useful historical precedents for linking the *Cairo Punch* to graphics by Zaghlul supporters after 1919 (definitely including Zaki himself). If we look at surviving lithographs from the first years after the *Cairo Punch* press left Egypt, Zaki seems to have turned to an entirely different genre—one suggesting, at least for the time, an "adaptation" to the prevailing winds of commercial opportunity.

Even though its physical operations were located in Italy beginning in 1908, the *Cairo* Punch continued contributing to the publishing market in Egypt. Its role as a politically engaged organ, however, underwent visible changes. For a number of years, it maintained an office address in Cairo—Number 2, Sharî'a 'Abd al-'Azîz). From there, a number of original lithographs, eventually including essentially "decorative" commemorative scenes or others depicting political topics very different from his 1907–1908 drawings, found their way into the local market. What is essential to note about these little-known lithographs is that, in contrast to the satirical and unmistakably anti-British tone of the *Cairo Punch*'s early issues, some motivating factor, perhaps something as mundane as the need to obtain a modest profit, led Zaki to promote subjects that one would not have expected from a publication bearing the label *Punch*.

"REAL PRECEDENTS"

Popular Nonpolitical/Nonsatirical Posters by the Cairo Punch *and Lesser-Known Lithographers*

Somewhat unexpectedly, only two out of more than twenty lithographs in a collection acquired in Egypt in 1948 by the British Museum were connected, and then only indirectly, with Egyptian subjects.[1] Most of the prints in the collection, many in the form of posters done by the *Cairo Punch* press between 1908 and 1914, deal with Ottoman imperial subjects, including symbolic representations of parliamentary or Islamic legitimacy. All are in distinct contrast to the strongly satirical political graphics associated with what Palmira Brummett labels "Ottoman Revolutionary" caricatures from the same period.[2]

Several things stand out in these little-known images that presage 'Abd al-Hamid Zaki's decision to introduce simple, often naïve folk imagery into his (apparently commercially distributed) lithographs. The Ka'ba scene in figure 5.1, for example, definitely contains artistic simplifications that could attract the appreciation of a popular, relatively unsophisticated viewership.

Surviving contemporary photographs confirm that all of the religiously significant elements in this scene by Zaki did in fact exist within and around the confines of the Ka'ba at the time. The configuration of landmarks is accurate, although the main religious buildings have been placed quite close together and brightly colored for maximal visual effect. The background area on the other hand, allowed more freedom for a simplified stylized approach. At the same time, care was taken to give prominent recognition to the Ottoman flag—something probably expected in more secular posters, perhaps less so here. The red banner with the single star and crescent appears both in the immediate background and in the stylized rendering of the holy site of Mount Arafat in the distance, where the artist's version of the traditional religious memorial on the summit lends it the contours of a fortress.

Introduction of simple symbols in this series of commemorative Islamic scenes is even more pronounced in figure 5.2, *The Egyptian and Syrian* Mahmals, *and Mohammedan Pilgrims at Monte Arafat.*[3] Although this 1910 poster appears to be the first by Zaki's press after having moved to Italy

MECCA AND THE GREAT HOLY MOSQUE : Mohammedan pilgrims going round the "KAABA. Nearly 400,000 pilgrims come from the Islamic World yearly to visit Mecca.

ALL RIGHTS RESERVED
"THE CAIRO PUNCH."

5.1. The Holy City of Mecca. © The Trustees of the British Museum.

alluding to Egypt's role as a "special" province of the Ottoman Empire, its content is still purely cere-monial. No political message, unless it be the recurring symbolic inclusion of the Ottoman imperial flag, seems to be implied. Artistic variations suggesting folk imagery are inserted, as are simple techniques to "liven" interest in subject matters predefined by ceremonial tradition. The widespread use of green, the traditional color of the Prophet, represented in the green Islamic banner beside the red Ottoman flag, for example, also appears in the robes of pilgrims in the foreground. One of these has a colorful green parasol, while a second carries a "complementary" red parasol. The same traditionally revered color stands out in the elaborate (red or green) decorations adorning the Syrian and Egyptian *maḥâmil* (pl.) facing the crowd. One can only venture the suggestion that the graphic splendor of Egypt's ceremonial contribution to the pilgrimage reflects Zaki's pride in the importance of his home province's support for the Islamic realm under protective Ottoman aus-pices. But such symbolic identification with Egypt would still have been far from any suggestion of its unique historical and political status or dilemmas created by the British occupation since 1882.[4]

Early elements of folk imagery seen in the *Egyptian and Syrian Mahmals* poster are carried forward in Zaki's 1911 poster *al-Ḥujâj Enter from the Bâb al-Salâm into the Holy Mosque at Madîna* (figure 5.3).[5] Several details here suggest that Zaki's use of symbolism was evolving from its initial quite elementary level and beginning to introduce secondary content implying simple political and secular social content. Indications appear in his representation of one individual in clearly Western attire in a group that included—in contrast to the traditionally clad majority—at least a half dozen men wearing effendi-style tarbush head gear. A single uniformed officer is prominent on the edge of the anonymous group scene as well. Inclusion of such unexpected details—absent from earlier stylistically simplified representations of "types"—also appeared in the *Egyptian and*

5.2. The Egyptian and Syrian *Mahmals* and Mohammedan Pilgrims at Monte Arafat. © The Trustees of the British Museum.

Syrian Mahmals poster. There, Zaki seems to have made an extra effort to personalize several pilgrims by providing realistic individual facial features. He also used his imagination in two other cases to suggest ethnic and sociocultural diversification (one African and one Chinese pilgrim—replete with queue) in the crowd of believers.

The *Cairo Punch* publisher definitely intended the 1911 *Bâb al-Salâm* poster (and probably other unpreserved graphics from the same period) to begin to say something more than what immediately met the eye. But for some reason it is only in figure 5.3 that he actually inserted a "statement of purpose" *in Arabic*, not marginally, but prominently placed at the center of the scene. The note announces (here in paraphrased translation) the beginning of the *Cairo Punch*'s fourth year of publication "after undergoing considerable difficulties." It promises "the introduction of important improvements . . without wavering in the honorable goal of . . . serving the beloved homeland and [bringing] enlightenment."

It is difficult in retrospect to know what this somewhat enigmatic statement might have been meant to communicate. Were "considerable difficulties"—financial perhaps—reflected in a need to print "simple" subjects, tapping a broader audience in order to sustain his press? Or did they stem from political circumstances affecting earlier, very different publication goals in Egypt that remain unknown? Service to what "homeland"?[6] Although there is no ready answer to such questions, it is possible that events in Egypt were beginning to rekindle Zaki's attention to the political scene he had earlier attempted to influence through satirical illustrations in the *Cairo Punch*. Even though the graphic framework for revisiting Egyptian topics remained tied to popular and religiously inspired subjects in 1911, a change in Zaki's use of such symbols was becoming

ALL RIGHTS RESERVED

5.3. Entry of the Pilgrims [al-ḥjâj] in Medina Through the Bab al-Salam. © The Trustees of the British Museum.

5.4. The Egyptian Maḥmal at Monte Arafat. © The Trustees of the British Museum.

apparent. On a personal level, for example, one particularly unique contemporary document is striking. When Zaki became a *ḥâjjî* by performing his pilgrimage obligation (probably in 1910, the year in which *Egyptian and Syrian Mahmals* was published) he commemorated the event by printing a portrait scene (figure 5.4) of himself with a group of rather notable fellow Egyptian pilgrims. The scene is an idealized scenario incorporating the ceremonial *maḥmil* with a typically crowded, stylized representation of Mount Arafat in the background.[7]

Popular Posters Focused on Egyptian Subjects

As stated, only a few lithographs in the British Museum's 1948 acquisition actually touch on Egyptian subjects. One, done later than most of the other prints, was a commemoration of Khedive ʿAbbas II's fateful mid-1914 visit to Istanbul just prior to the outbreak of World War I.[8] Britain's imposition of protectorate status over Egypt a few months later, followed by the forced deposition ʿAbbas, marked the beginning of the khedive's years of exile. As a political statement, this particular poster rather obviously complements the posters Zaki did in the immediate years after 1908 emphasizing support for the Istanbul Sultanate. Its emphasis on the sultan's official reception of the khedive essentially as his peer, however, may indicate Zaki's already changing attitude toward the Egyptian homeland (*al-waṭan al-ʿazîz*, "the Great Fatherland," written into figure 5.3's "pledge"?), which he had left six years earlier.

Somewhat earlier, chronologically datable signs of the re-identification of the *Cairo Punch* press with Egypt's political circumstances appear in two other commemorative posters. These

5.5. H. H. Hadji Abbas Helmi II, Kedive [*sic*] of Egypt at Madina. Courtesy of Nehal El-Naggar.

were undoubtedly also meant to emphasize—albeit indirectly—the importance of 'Abbas II's leadership of Egyptian pilgrims during the 1911 hajj. They definitely went beyond simple, general ceremonial scenes to personalize the central figure of the khedive. Figure 5.5, *H. H. Hadji Abbas Helmi II, Khedive of Egypt at Madina*, is replete with symbols of pomp and circumstance worthy of what one might expect of a representation of the sultan himself.[9]

The scene underlines the presence of several high military figures in the company of the khedive, a military honor guard, and an elite military band. But equally impressive, beyond the usual symbols of imperial-red and Islamic-green flags, are looming images meant to symbolize 'Abbas's (and therefore Egypt's) association with signs of the material and technological progress brought to the holy cities of the Hijaz under the aegis of the Ottoman Sultanate. Symbols of this progress are openly declared by bold representations of the (Damascus to Medina) Hijaz railway and newly introduced electric power lines connecting the Hijaz to distant Syria.[10]

Figure 5.6 is quite different, showing the khedive in the traditional garb worn by all *ḥujâj* and accompanied by several (probably Egyptian) personalities who would have been identifiable, like 'Abbas himself, by their detailed facial features. All are following the closely defined procedures that guide the ceremonial stages of the pilgrimage.[11]

In this drawing, suggesting the ideal equality of believers no matter what their social or political rank, Zaki edges even closer to expanding elements of folk imagery introduced in other, much simpler depictions of familiar Islamic scenes. The seemingly isolated figure of one person in Western clothing stands out (near one other tarbush wearer), in contrast to the majority of robe-bearing and traditionally turbaned onlookers or the few individuals wearing the headdress characteristic of the Arabian Peninsula.

5.6. H. H. Hadji Abbas Helmi II, Khedive of Egypt at Mecca. Courtesy of Nehal El-Naggar.

The main point here is that, while these "transitional" lithographs maintain reverence for Islamic religious traditions, they now draw attention to Egypt's important provincial identity and the figure of the Khedive of Egypt himself as a symbol of political leadership. At the same time, symbols conveying common social themes—signs of material progress in figure 5.5, for example—and sartorial, hence social, diversity in figure 5.6, are beginning to lend themselves, like the *Images d'Épinal* seen in an earlier chapter, to the "everyday" nature of the composition. In both cases, sentiments of pride, however simple, are conveyed to the viewer.

"Pure" Folk Imagery by Egyptian Lithographers: Popular "Keepsake" Posters[12]

Both the JWM/Utah and the LL/Cairo collections also hold a small number of original and quite definitely *nonpolitical* Egyptian lithographs. These examples are of particular interest: the names of their essentially unknown artists are printed on them—along with that of fellow "keepsake" artist 'Abd al-Hamid Zaki. A number of these same names also appear on the Wafd political posters printed after 1918. This may mean that such local artist-printers and the "keepsake" genre either led the *Cairo Punch*'s founder *or* followed him in producing almost identical political posters with much the same popular folk imagery and symbols during the Wafd's first election campaign.

Internal evidence in some of the "keepsake" graphics indicates they were printed before, but not long before, World War I, when few in Egypt—possibly even the several artists who did them—could imagine a coming popular election. Therefore, when someone decided to print colorful posters supporting Saad Zaghlul's candidacy, it could well have been the scarcely known artists in these small shops who chose the content and artistic style that emerged in the work that began to appear. Still, because we definitely find *Cairo Punch* artist/publisher 'Abd al-Hamid Zaki (already with a full decade of experience as a creator of politically motivated graphics) engaged in this pre-1918 "keepsake" market, it seems likely he was the one spearheading the Wafd campaign posters project, as well as the style they adopted.

What evidence remains to suggest the number and nature of small shops producing illustrations for a modest popular-art market in Egypt in this period? With the notable exception of prints traceable to Zaki's *Cairo Punch*, the printers who produced such popular materials were *not* involved at the same time as journalists. Their prints were intended for direct sale as part of shop production, individual subscription, or on market stands and kiosks. These rarely bore any secular symbolism, and even less frequently, political themes. Their subject matter usually commemorated popular Islamic scenes with strong emphasis on folk imagery. The examples in figures 5.7 and 5.8, one done by the *Cairo Punch* press and the other by the Cairene printer Ahmad Za'zû', are part of that broad category. Given the limited number of surviving originals, one can only venture the suggestion that, since this type of graphic was probably intended for decoration in modest private residences, subject matter almost always celebrated popular cultural tableaux. Figures 5.7 and 5.8 are quite distinct from open political graphics such as the *Cairo Punch*'s 1914 depiction of Sultan Mahmud V with 'Abbas II, even though the khedive's presence in such settings could be taken equally as a symbol of his deference to religious tradition or as an "official" commemorative event. In all events, religiously relevant themes prevail in all the pre-1914 examples of the keepsake genre that found their way into the JWM/Utah and LL/Cairo collections. These themes are either Old Testament in origin (i.e., falling within the Judeo-Christian-Muslim "People of the Book" framework recognized by Islam) or purely Islamic in content. Again, no discernible political polemic motivated the artists or publishers whose purpose was essentially to profit from the sale of such popular decorative prints.

Examples that have survived may be of interest less for their well-known subjects than for their artistic styles. Each contains elements of folk imagery intended to please relatively unsophisticated viewers. This may already play some role in leading us toward the provenance of the Wafd political posters that, within a few years, would be designed and printed by the same presses that produced the popular imagery characteristic of the keepsake market.

Figures 5.7 and 5.8 depicting Abraham facing the Angel of God while preparing to sacrifice Isaac are stylistically quite similar. Despite the very summary representation of the natural setting with mountains and diverse vegetation in both posters, the physical features and proportions of both human and animal subjects are drawn with considerable attention to detail, presumably to demonstrate the technical skills of the two artists. Figure 5.7 is a product of the *Cairo Punch* press; figure 5.8 was drawn by Ahmad Za'zû'.

A different level of both folk imagery and symbolism derived from religious tradition appears in three other decorative graphics. One (figure 5.9) is also by Ahmad Za'zû', while two others (figures 5.10 and 5.11) were printed by Muhammad 'Ali al-Jundi. Al-Jundi, like Za'zû' (individually and as part of a group that founded, somewhere near this time the Sharika Surûr Wataniyya (Partnership, or Company of/for Nationalist Illustrations) was also later among the Egyptian printers who did posters supporting the Wafd.[13]

As in the illustrations of Abraham preparing for the sacrifice, these posters are based either on specific scriptural verses (extracts from which appear on both depictions of the Ark), or in the case of al-Burâq ("Lighting," the steed that bore Muhammad on his night ascent from Jerusalem), multiple references in the *hadîth* literature.

All Rights Reserved "THE CAIRO PUNCH" Cairo (Egypt)

◄ الأدارة : رقم ٢ ميدان البيدق بشارع عبد العزيز بمصر ◄ سيدنا ابراهيم الخليل حينما اراد ان يضحي ولده سيدنا اسمعيل فاتاه الملاك بكبش قداه

ان هذا لهو البلاء المبين وفديناه بذبح عظيم

5.7. (TOP) Abraham's Sacrifice (I)
5.8. (BOTTOM) Abraham's Sacrifice (II)
Both images courtesy of Special Collections, J. Willard Marriott Library, University of Utah.

5.9. (TOP) Noah's Ark (I)

5.10. (BOTTOM) Noah's Ark (II); Duplicate of Figure 3.3

Both images courtesy of Special Collections, J. Willard Marriott Library, University of Utah.

5.11. Al-Burâq of the Noble Prophet (in Arabic). Courtesy of Special Collections, J. Willard Marriott Library, University of Utah.

Both al-Jundi's representation of Noah's Ark, and, to a somewhat lesser degree, Za'zû''s version of same, contain stylistic elements inspired by folk imagery. In figure 5.10, al-Jundi gives full rein to his imagination with minimal concern for realism. The multitude of human figures, with the exception of Noah himself and his wife, are essentially anonymous and—given the lack of any attempt to draw individual personal features—reproduce nearly identical facial features. On the other hand, great care was taken to distinguish the many different animal species crowded on the ark. It is here that the artist's hand—intentionally or not—created imagery that could easily qualify the poster as folk art. In many cases, reverence associated with a scriptural subject yields to a temptation to provide innocent amusement through folk imagery—for example, the human figure in the foreground petting a rabbit while the fox at his side eyes a vulnerable mouse, or the figure of a goose comfortably installed on the head of a docile elephant. If one looks closely at the naïve drawings of any of the individual animals, a similar effect emerges: idealized rendering of the innate character of each species endears all the animals to the viewer.

In the Noah's Ark poster by Ahmad Za'zû' (figure 5.9), there is more detailed emphasis on Noah and family, including his sons and their wives. One can presume it is Noah's veiled wife who holds what may be the dictate from God to build the Ark. On the other hand, Za'zû''s rendering of a small collection of single-gender animals aboard the Ark (mainly larger mammal species and birds, unlike the more diverse and frequently *drôle* menagerie in al-Jundi's picture) reflects much the same attention to naturalistic detail seen in his drawing of Abraham's sacrifice.

In figure 5.11, a second example of a popular lithograph by Muhammad al-Jundi, the artist was again able to exercise extensive imagination. Here he incorporates several colorful symbols into

5.12. Delilah Cutting Samson's Locks. Courtesy of Special Collections, J. Willard Marriott Library, University of Utah.

his drawing of al-Burâq, the steed who bore Muhammad during the Night Journey (*al-mi'râj*), or the Prophet's ascension to heaven.[14] A degree of fantasy appears in the artist's rendering of an opulently decorated Burâq. The horse is depicted with the head of a jewel-bedecked woman—something often repeated in the extensive iconography associated with al-Burâq. To this, al-Jundi adds simple symbolic elements: a small sketch of the K'ba in Mecca where the Night Journey began, a pure white moon in the nocturnal sky, and a roughly sketched conception of angelic onlookers bearing flowers.

A third small-scale Egyptian printer was Ibrahim 'Ikrîsha. He too produced several similar keepsake lithographs based on popular religious tradition, was a participating member of the Company for National[ist] Illustrations mentioned above, and later contributed to the Wafd poster campaign. All three of 'Ikrîsha's lithographs in the Marriott Library collection develop different events taken from the story of Samson, originally drawn from the Old Testament Book of Judges. Although the figure of Samson does not appear in the Qur'an, tracts by prominent Islamic scholars, most notably al-Tabarî and al-Tha'alibî, recognized his importance to Islam—again through the revered medium of the *hadîth* literature. Figure 5.12 offers the artist's interpretation of one key phase of Delilah's betrayal of Samson to Philistine enemies seeking to overcome his impressive strength. Here, Delilah is seen cutting Samson's locks, the assumed source of his physical power.

Compared with other keepsake lithographs in the JWM/Utah and LL/Cairo collections, 'Ikrîsha's drawings depicting the story of Samson are somewhat less attentive to finished details. But they share a common feature: use of simple folk imagery appreciable by any viewer to convey the popular drama of the subject.

All Rights Reserved "THE CAIRO PUNCH" Cairo (Egypt)

5.13. ʿAntara ibn Shaddâd Defeats Rabîʿ ibn al-Muqattam. Courtesy of Special Collections, J. Willard Marriott Library, University of Utah.

The last two keepsake posters preserved in the JWM/Utah collection reflect specific Islamic traditions handed down from both pre-Islamic times and the early era of the Muslim community. Both were printed by ʿAbd al-Hamid Zaki's *Cairo Punch* press.

Figure 5.13 depicts the tradition of the pre-Islamic hero and poet ʿAntar ibn Shaddâd defeating his rival tribal enemy Rabîʿ ibn al-Muqattam and his cohorts. Here one might say that typical folk imagery is transformed into spectacular form: violent battle scenes in this tradition are meant to leave little to the imagination!

The second poster, figure 5.14, commemorates (future Caliph) ʿAlî ibn Abî Ṭâlib's victorious struggle in the Battle of the Trench against the champion of the enemy Quraysh forces Amr ibn ʿAbd al-Wudd al-ʿAmrî. These two posters, replete with sanguine depictions of limb severing and violent decapitation, nonetheless follow the general tenets of symbolism in folk imagery: heroism and the victory of good over evil.[15] The elementary yet spectacular graphic style here, including ʿAmrî's calm but defiant face as he raises his severed leg in the battle scene in figure 5.14, is complemented by simple symbolism in the background, where totally stylized, colorful pyramid shapes represent the Muslim encampment. Additional symbolism appears in the quite unexpected placement of the star-and-crescent flag of the twentieth-century Ottoman Empire alongside the green banner of the Prophet in a historical scene drawn from the seventh century CE!

Only one lithograph in the keepsake genre (presumably done in this same prewar, pre-Wafd period by Ahmad Zaʿzûʿ) can be called a harbinger of what became the politically motivated poster work produced by Egyptian presses after 1918.[16] Figure 5.15 is a totally imaginative scene

5.14. ʿAlî ibn Abî Tâlib's Victory at the Battle of the Trench. Courtesy of Special Collections, J. Willard Marriott Library, University of Utah.

portraying the "rescue" of a tightly bound female figure representing Egypt from the depths of the Nile. The background is Cairo, replete with Pyramids, the dominant Qalʿa fortress, associated mosques, and a very simplified representation of a Pharaonic temple. Although it is difficult to assign more than symbolic identity to the equally idealized male prisoner on the river bank, one can assume that the impressive noble figure who stands beside him (with the caption "The hero of Egypt orders his men to save her") probably stands symbolically for the legitimate authority responsible for protecting Egypt's right to self-rule.[17] For whatever reason, the artist depicts the rescuers as black Africans, perhaps suggesting their status as slaves owned by the obviously highly placed individual identified as the Hero of Egypt.

When the Wafd movement after 1918 laid claim to responsibility for overseeing Egypt's needs, Zaʿzûʿ, ʿAbd al-Hamid Zaki, and other printers of political propaganda posters put Saad Zaghlul's personal image in the place of such idealized "traditional" guarantors of the country's fate. Between the two periods, however, there was a need to prepare both artistic and political steps that could lead from pre-1914 nationalist symbols—particularly those associated with the earlier Watanist group—to the emergent independence claims championed by the Wafd. Chance discovery of a lithographic poster combining political claims with what I have called the "missing-link" graphic style in Egyptian political caricatures once again assigns a key role in that preparation to *Cairo Punch* publisher ʿAbd al-Hamid Zaki.

5.15. Egypt Rescued from Assailants on the Nile. Courtesy of Lesley Lababidy.

In Memory of the Late Mustafa Kamel Pasha:
A Prototypic Transfer from Ottoman to Egyptian Political Caricature

The dozen or so nonpolitical posters discussed up to this point confirm that *Cairo Punch* editor 'Abd al-Hamid Zaki and several other printers in Egypt sold various popular lithographs in the decade before World War I. Yet Zaki seems to have been the only Egyptian lithographer with a cumulative experience—ranging from the openly satirical pages of his 1907–1908 *Cairo Punch* through several years working with Ottoman propaganda themes—who could have prepared his press in particular to print different types of politically engaged graphics. Hints that he might have been predisposed in the prewar years to return to specifically Egyptian political subjects already appeared when he focused on the khedive's participation in the hajj, then on 'Abbas's ill-fated 1914 official visit to Istanbul. Apparently, none of the other Egyptian lithographers who shared the minor keepsake market in this period experimented with scenes containing even indirect reference to Egypt's particular political or cultural status within the Ottoman Empire. Zaki, however, was quite prepared to do so.

A very significant and quite different poster in the British Museum's 1948 special acquisition, *In Memory of the Late Mustafa Kamel*, (figure 5.16) makes it clear that after 1908 Zaki never ceased to support Egypt's political claims against the British occupation.[18] It also suggests that Zaki's adoption of the "Ottoman mold" after leaving his earlier satirical work behind was going to serve him (and other local graphic artists) once full "Egyptianizing" of the medium of political posters came to serve Saad Zaghlul's cause after 1918.

5.16. In Memory of the Late Moustafa Kamel Pasha. © The Trustees of the British Museum.

Given the approximate date—probably 1912—when Zaki completed *In Memory*, it should not be surprising that he chose Watan Party founder Mustafa Kamil and two individuals (already open rivals living in exile outside Egypt) who claimed to be his successors as focal subjects. What is striking about this poster is, first, that it may be the only surviving graphic during the period between moving the *Cairo Punch* press to Italy and taking up the Wafd cause after World War I in which Zaki made an unambiguous statement about Egypt's difficult political situation. Second, figure 5.16, although openly political, is an early example of Zaki's use of an artistic style that was quite different from anything, either in his previous (1907–1908) satirical work, propaganda posters done in his (post–1908) "Ottoman Period," or in the keepsake graphics reviewed earlier. More than anything else, figure 5.16 recalls the style used by artists supporting the already apparently distant memory of Ottoman constitutional "victories" in 1876 and 1908.

To substantiate this suggestion, one should compare figure 5.16 with figures 3.7 and 3.8, both done earlier by anonymous artists, probably in Istanbul. Both use symbolism and folk imagery similar to Zaki's commemoration of the deceased founder of Egypt's Watan movement. The rare *In Memory* poster, therefore, suggests that the *Cairo Punch* press was already in a position before World War I to adopt preexisting, highly simplified Ottoman prototypes and folk imagery to attract supporters to the Wafd as the Ottoman Empire faced final dismantlement.

Several features visible in figure 5.16 continue the symbolic content seen in many of Zaki's earlier posters, including the stereotypic presence of male effendi figures in the crowd surrounding Kamil (one sees only two turban-clad persons beyond the enigmatic figure of Shaykh 'Abd al-'Aziz Shawish himself) and the recurring symbols of red and green banners.[19] Beyond several written slogans proclaiming in very simple terms the Watanist (and then several years later, the Wafd) goals, this poster presents another caricatured image of a female personifying Egypt herself.[20] Here Egypt appears to be awaiting (either in symbolic slumber or in modest passivity, and dressed in what appears to be typical rural village attire) determined action from expected political liberators—the triad of Watan Party figures.

On a different level of symbolism, this image reflects a problem notable in earlier Ottoman posters that carries over to later Egyptian graphics reviewed in the next chapter: how to represent "everyday" women supporters of male political leaders and their cause. Despite its apparent inspiration from earlier Ottoman models, in Zaki's *In Memory* the question seems to be skirted entirely: while Egypt as an idealized female figure awaits liberation, there is no other woman in the scene.

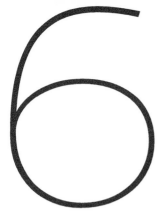

WAFD POLITICAL POSTERS, 1919–1923

A Culmination of Preexisting Symbolism and Folk Imagery

A review of original lithographs in the WJM/Utah and LL/Cairo Wafd campaign poster collection determines the extent to which they combine Egyptian folk imagery and symbolism with what Afaf Marsot considered a chief attribute of all cartoon (as well as caricature) drawings. "A cartoon," she wrote in 1971, "purports to reveal the 'reality' behind a public figure or a situation, but a reality which is in fact a distortion designed . . . for the . . . purpose of influencing the spectator."[1]

For the sake of more or less systematic organization, the posters in this chapter are considered in several groups, each reflecting what appears to be a "'reality' behind . . . a situation . . . designed . . . [to influence] the spectator."[2] This division is not meant to suggest that at the time of their original work the artists were consciously following a set of didactic priorities. We have no way of knowing whether individual lithographers sought to stress one or another of the subjective themes separated here for the sake of organizational convenience. There seems to have been some consensus among them, however, that a certain number of subject areas justified emphasis to gain the public's attention during the Wafd's campaign, since several artists returned to quite similar themes more than once.

Despite the elementary nature of the symbolism and folk imagery employed, there are some notable differences between the work of different artists who drew posters for the Wafd campaign. None were visibly engaged in "copying" previous or contemporaneous work produced by 'Abd al-Hamid Zaki's *Cairo Punch* press. In fact, even given its highly visible role, at least in numbers of posters produced, the *Cairo Punch* sometimes fell behind other lesser-known lithographers in presenting new and original subjects in different ways.

Although only two examples of "official" lithograph portraits appeared in earlier chapters—the early wartime portrait of Sultan Mehmet V (figure 3.9) and an undated formal image of Saad Zaghlul (figure 2.1), their inclusion seemed appropriate at those particular points for similar reasons. First, if figure 3.9 is compared with other representations of Mehmed V from the same period, it is fairly clear that tradition demanded that the artist replicate the sultan's features without any change of facial expression from portrait to portrait. The same is true for almost all the portrait posters of Saad Zaghlul reproduced here. His expression remains sober and all artists typically reproduced *near identical* details in all portraits of the Raʾīs's face.

Something similar applies to matters of attire, which is formal in all cases. In the sultan's portraits, of course, imperial protocol demanded that, if there were any sartorial differences from one representation to another, they could only reflect differences in official uniforms. No subjective choice was left to the artist. Again, with only minor exceptions, a similar rigidity guided artists' rendering of Zaghlul's attire. It had by necessity to reflect his social rank as a member of the elite Westernized class, with no chance variations in sartorial style. He always appears in the Wafd campaign posters with the inevitable red tarbush marking effendi status and near-identical black suits. Almost all portraits present Zaghlul face on, with only minor variations in posture to accommodate different activities in the few scenarios presented here.

Given such stereotypic constraints, the viewer must look beyond the portrait itself for signs of the lithographer's message. These usually depend on quite simple symbols accompanying the central figure. In the case of Sultan Mehmed's portraits, for example, symbols are obvious. Surrounded (in figure 3.9) by miniature images of at least fifteen of his predecessors, the continuity of the sultan's authority is visibly proclaimed. Then, two inset scenes of military activities attest to the power he represents.

Representations of Zaghlul occasionally incorporate elements of folk imagery coming from the lithographers' imagination that are much less apparent and probably intended to carry simple messages to unsophisticated viewers. The *Cairo Punch* image of the Wafd leader in figure 6.1—essentially duplicated in all his portrait posters in the JWM/Utah collections—is accompanied by a typically brief honorific caption. The phrase "*ṣâḥib al-mʿâlî*" here, for example, traditionally translates as "His Excellency."

Two incidental, distinguishing symbols appear in this portrait: the newly devised *three*-star Egyptian flag and the slogan written on the folded paper in Zaghlul's hand, "You must be unified, O sons of the glorious nation, for [unity] is the great force that [will lead us to] complete independence."

The second portrait (figure 6.2, which lacks an identifiable provenance) is more specific, stating that he is "writing the history of the Egyptian awakening (*al-nahḍa al-miṣriyya*)." Particularly important in this portrait is its suggestion of Zaghlul's continuing symbolic dependence on earlier figures whose "shadows" of influence he probably would have preferred to avoid in the Wafd's initial election bid—but not yet. The three portraits on the wall—Watan Party founder Mustafa Kamil and his presumed (but clearly controversial) successors—introduce a paradox here and in several other posters.[3] They associate the Wafd's paramount leader with personalities who actually never collaborated with his movement. Mustafa Kamil's antioccupation activities before his death in 1908 occurred when Zaghlul was still safely ensconced in ministerial service. Muhammad Farid remained, between 1911 and his death *in Berlin* in 1919, a political exile who never actually recognized Zaghlul's leadership of the nationalist cause after 1918.[4] An even more problematic case is that of Shaykh ʿAbd al-ʿAziz Shawish, who was also in exile (and roundly

(كافة الحقوق محفوظه لجريدة السياسة المصوره عدد ٢٣٤) صاحب المعالي سعد باشا زغلول   All Rights Reserved "THE CAIRO PUNCH" Cairo (Egypt)

6.1. His Excellency Saad Pasha Zaghlul. Courtesy of Special Collections, J. Willard Marriott Library, University of Utah.

rejected time after time by Farid) when this poster was printed. He would only return to Egypt *after* the Wafd's first electoral success and despite Zaghlul's apparent reluctance to receive him. There is ample documentation suggesting that Shawish fit neither Farid's definition of Egypt's nationalist cause nor what the creators of these posters assumed was Zaghlul's recognition of his political importance.[5] But, for purposes of reassuring potential supporters that the Wafd was continuing the cause of the Watan Party (and thus justified in recruiting some of its members into its ranks), the symbolism here can definitely be considered, a temporary "reality," and (to quote Afaf Marsot once again) "a distortion designed ... for the ... purpose of influencing the spectator."

6.2. His Excellency the Leader . . . Writing the History of the Egyptian Awakening. Courtesy of Special Collections, J. Willard Marriott Library, University of Utah.

Symbolism in the last "official" Zaghlul portrait reviewed here (figure 6.3, lithographer and printer again unknown) is easier to understand. The individuals whose portraits surround Zaghlul here were all well-known representatives of the Islamic religious establishment, although three of the four were deceased by the time the poster was printed. By far the most famous were Sayyid Jamal al-Din al-Afghani (1839–1897) and Shaykh Muhammad ʿAbduh (1849–1905), in the upper left and upper right corners respectively.[6] The lower two turbaned religious figures, on the other hand, could at least have been associated, in the eyes of a few well-informed viewers, with the changing political situation after 1918. "The late Ustadh Shaykh Muhammad Ismaʿil al-Bardisi" (lower right corner) served only six months (July–December, 1920, the very early months of the Wafd's call for unity behind Zaghlul) as appointed head (i.e., "state" mufti) of the Dâr al-Iftâ.[7] As a youth, al-Bardisi had apparently frequented circles surrounding Jamal al-Din al-Afghani. Thus, once again, inclusion of his portrait here could have been meant to suggest, albeit indirectly, an attitude of support from the higher ranks of the Egyptian ʿulamâʾ with some history of political involvement.

But inclusion of the fourth ʿâlim, Shakh Mustafa al-Qayâtî (lower left), the one living contemporary among the four who could actually have been considered a follower of the Wafd's initial activities, leaves no doubt that the Wafd was anxious to publicize an active religious spokesman's overt adherence to its cause. A number of sources mention, but do not name, members of the religious establishment as participants in the pro-Wafdist demonstrations after 1918. Al-Qayâtî's role as a Wafd supporter, however, stood out prominently and regularly. This led to his appointment for a time as a member of the party's executive committee. Although this case of personal support from al-Qayâtî was exceptional, his presence in a poster like this one fits the general theme concerning symbolism in "official" portraits of Saad Zaghlul. The artist-propagandist implies that representatives of the Islamic religious establishment generally approve of the Wafd by progressive advance from distant and only indirect symbols (al-Afghani and ʿAbduh) to a specific contemporary actor (al-Qayâtî) in its ongoing campaign.

This search for legitimacy by association appears in the next portrait as well (figure 6.4). This lithograph is identified as the work of "Ibrahim ʿIkrîsha and his associates."[8] Here, the image of Prince ʿUmar Tusun appears alongside the same three former Watan Party leaders represented in figure 6.2. Prince Tusun, in contrast to Kamil, Farid, and Shaykh Shawish, had by 1920 actually given the impression of moving over from earlier association with the Watanists to play an active, if sometimes unpredictable, part in the Wafdist movement. Tusun's publicly visible role as a supporter of the Wafd's cause would lead to his repeated appearance in a considerable number of posters discussed in later sections of this chapter.

Internal evidence in figure 6.4 helps assign an approximate date. An inserted medallion associating the four august personalities with the original design model for Egyptian artist Mahmud Mukhtar's statue Nahḍa Miṣr (Egypt's Awakening) suggests the drawing may have been done in 1920 or shortly thereafter.[9] The figure of the Sphinx in this ensemble became essential in the pharaonic symbolism used by many nationalist illustrators over the years in different graphic contexts.[10]

The Enigma of Mr. Swan:
The Sole (and Openly Friendly) Englishman "Adopted" by Saad Zaghlul

Any attempt to apply to these portraits Marsot's definition of cartoons/caricatures as realities "behind a public figure . . . , but . . . in fact a distortion designed . . . [to influence] the spectator" is of course conjectural. A last, quite unexpected, example of formal portraiture of the Raʾîs is

6.3. Zaghlul and Portraits of Religious Scholar Supporters. Courtesy of Special Collections, J. Willard Marriott Library, University of Utah.

6.4. Zaghlul and (Presumed) Wafdist Supporters with the 1920 Mukhtar Statue. Courtesy of Special Collections, J. Willard Marriott Library, University of Utah.

particularly challenging in this respect. Figure 6.5, by Zaʿzûʿ's Sharika Ṣurûr Waṭaniyya places the unchanging portrait of Zaghlul next to the only person in "everyday" western attire (including hat and shirt collar) and the sole image of an Englishman in the JWM/Utah and LL/Cairo collections.

The Englishman's portrait, appearing comfortably at ease beside Zaghlul, bears a simple name: Mister Swan. Further research yielded some information concerning the biography of Mister Swan but no definite clue as to why he appears beside the founder of the Wafd. George Swan would have been to some degree identifiable—but certainly not to the average Egyptian, nor even to typical British subjects—as the author of *Lacked Ye Anything?*, a historical account of the activities of the Egyptian General Mission.[11] Swan had been a member of the British Protestant mission program in Egypt since the early years after 1900 and was important enough to replace mission head Arthur T. Upson during the latter's temporary absence from Egypt in 1908.

Since Zaghlul was serving as minister of education between 1906 and 1909, this might explain how he made the acquaintance of Swan, through the latter's involvement with the General Mission's schools. Still, a possible "business" association, even if it may have been augmented by some form of personal interaction, does not really explain why the Wafd poster artists chose

6.5. Zaghlul ... and "Mister Swan." Courtesy of Special Collections, J. Willard Marriott Library, University of Utah.

"Mister Swan" as somehow vaguely symbolizing his personal support of their cause. It seems unlikely, for example, that Zaghlul would have chosen to identify publicly with a Protestant Christian mission to signal his approval of freedom of religion or intersectarian cooperation of any sort. With only a few exceptions, the posters that have survived suggest that issues of religion touching the Islamic majority or Christian minority in Egypt were not chosen as primary images for public distribution. Why Ahmad Zaʿzûʿs press chose to place Swan's portrait beside Zaghlul *without any caption* at all remains, therefore, something of a mystery.

Ironically, perhaps, the only symbolism one might venture to assign to the representation of Mister Swan may involve a "reverse positive" effect. The Wafd's obvious confrontation with the British was never openly expressed in these propaganda posters. There is not one drawing—not even a satirical caricature of a "friendly" John Bull—aiming at what would have been a logical target for anticolonial illustrators.[12] Perhaps to give the impression that the Wafd had no desire to encourage anti-British animosity, the subject was avoided altogether.[13] Or, as may be the case here, George Swan's image could have been included to draw attention to individuals in the British community whose position vis-a-vis high-level political negotiations was more or less neutral. Thus, perhaps this mysterious portrait comes closest to offering "a distortion of reality" in the sense of Marsot's quoted phrase. Who could possibly assume, however, that a highly placed Christian missionary was not concerned about Britain's political maneuverings in Egypt?

Commemoration of Specific Events in the Wafd's Bid for Political Recognition

The JWM/Utah and LL/Cairo collections contain three posters commemorating actual events that occurred either before Zaghlul's April 1921 return to Egypt following unsuccessful

6.6. Saad Zaghlul's April 1921 Return from First Exile. Courtesy of Special Collections, J. Willard Marriott Library, University of Utah.

Anglo-Egyptian negotiations, or later, after August 1922, when Safiya Zaghlul was permitted to join her husband during his second, long (January 1922–September 1923) period of exile. All of these contain symbolism and some elements of folk imagery. They are particularly notable for depiction of various social groups, especially Egyptian women of different rank, traditional "countryfolk," and effendi supporters of the Wafd.

Figure 6.6, one of only a few printed by the shop of Ahmad al-Shubkî in Cairo, shows the enthusiastic reception that greeted Zaghlul when he returned to Egypt from London in April 1921. Whether the conspicuous cavalcade actually did pass by the well-known Continental Hotel, the artist's use of this setting would have been considered very apt for its symbolic importance.[14] Located at the edge of Cairo's Opera Square, the Continental (then the Continental-Savoy) overlooks the famous equestrian statue of Ibrahim Pasha, son of Muhammad ʿAli and military governor of Syria during the 1830s. The hotel was also known as one of the most important stopping places for foreign dignitaries in Cairo. The fact that it served as a gathering place for highly placed Egyptians as well as foreigners, however, does not seem to have been the artist's only concern for creating a symbolic scene. Almost all the hotel windows are filled with highly simplified figures of Egyptian men wearing tarbushes and effendi apparel. Most of these are accompanied by very traditionally veiled women.

6.7. Zaghlul Departing for Malta and Second Exile. Courtesy of Special Collections, J. Willard Marriott Library, University of Utah.

In contrast to their veiled counterparts, there are three couples (plus one window occupied by a single woman) in which the women are hatless, with their hair, though scarcely visible, arranged in western-style curls. While all women in the poster are viewing events from the somewhat distant windows, the jubilant crowd of men in the street is mixed between effendi types and four traditional *galabiyya*-clad men, only one of whom is actually involved in open celebration. There are also two military officers in dress uniform.

Additional symbolism includes many flag-bearers, plus the equestrian statue of Ibrahim Pasha himself, and especially the presence in the automobile of the single most represented presumed supporter of Zaghlul, Prince ʿUmar Tusun. Inclusion of Tusun here may or may not have been historically accurate, since the Prince's record of behind-the-scenes political maneuvering, not always to the benefit of the Wafd, was well-known (but probably only to informed parties) in this same period.

Figure 6.7, which lacks any indication of the shop that printed it, can be dated any time after Zaghlul's first "detention" (*ḥuṣûr* in the caption) in 1919, when he was deported in the first stage by sea (here apparently on an Italian ship) to Malta. Like the imagined version of Zaghlul's "triumphant" return from inconclusive negotiations in April 1921, this poster takes a certain amount of liberty in setting the scene. Individuals watching the Wafd's supporters are mixed between effendis and countryfolk. Again, only one of the latter, however, is actually participating.

Three figures are worthy of special note, two as participants and one as a passive onlooker. A man and a woman beside the automobile are dressed in full Western attire. The woman may, but probably does not, represent Safiya Zaghlul, even though Mrs. Zaghlul was publicly associated with the Wafd cause from the outset. It is true that poster artists as well as photographers in this period tended to picture the Ra'is's *wife* dressed in Western styles. The woman pictured here wears Western clothing that only a minority of Egyptian women at the time might have chosen for special occasions. She is dressed in a colored blouse, skirt, and a stylish hat, while the man behind her sports what appears to be a boater style straw hat—(definitely *not* in keeping with her husband's or his associates' sartorial taste, if this caricature was originally meant to be a representation of Safiya Zaghlul! The only other woman, accompanied by two men in a small boat far from the main action, is veiled and wears the traditional black robe of conservative women. Drawn in "miniature," she gives the impression (like the women in the windows of the Continental Hotel in figure 6.6) of a passive onlooker, even though her boat flies the same Egyptian flag that is prominently displayed front and center. Viewers of either of these two commemorative posters would perhaps have had difficulty knowing, therefore, whether the Wafd wanted to identify its program with male and female *affandiyya* elements or with more traditional sectors of Egypt's post-1918 society.

Figure 6.8 portrays Safiya Zaghlul's departure from Egypt in October 1922 to join her husband during his second deportation. If one considers Beth Baron's account of this event, based on contemporary sources and photographs, it appears that the artist may have had mixed objectives in arranging the scene. Baron cites evidence, for example, that in November 1922 Zaghlul sent a letter from exile commending the founder and publisher of *al-Nahḍa al-Nisâʾiyya*, Labiba Ahmad, for the nationalist activities of her group, the Society of Egyptian Ladies' Awakening—this, despite the openly Islamic tendencies of her association.[15] The letter came just one month after Ahmad apparently "took center stage in demonstrations surrounding Safiya Zaghlul's departure from Cairo" (the very scene depicted here) under very different circumstances than in figure 6.8. In Baron's words, based on Ahmad's own published account,

> At the Cairo . . . station, Labiba presented Safiya with a Qurʾan . . . a book of blessings (*Dalâʾil al-Khayrât*), and a list of women and girls who had pledged on the Qurʾan to support . . . complete independence for Egypt and the Sudan. Labiba consciously infused her participation in the ritual send-off with Islamic symbolism.[16]

Could this implication of strong Islamic undertones accompanying Labiba's highly publicized recruitment of support for Madame Zaghlul at the time of her departure explain not only why there is no hint in figure 6.8 of any "special" celebration beyond calm flag waving by the restricted crowd in the drawing but also why Madame Zaghlul is the only woman in the picture?

The most striking visual aspect of this poster is, of course, the artist's placement in the foreground of a bigger-than-life Safiya Zaghlul, described in the caption as the "Ra'is" [*sic.*, correct Ar. feminine is *ra'isa*], and "sole leader." She is alone in the vehicle, except for her driver, and dressed entirely in Western clothing with a Western-style hair arrangement. Secondly, although there is a hint of diversity in the all-male crowd of well-wishers, including individuals in traditional *galabiyya*-like clothing, only three of these in the distant background have turban headwear. The few in the foreground are pictured with the same effendi symbol of the tarbush.

صفية زغلول

إلا احتفال محر يى الريّسى عند صفرها

6.8. Safiya Zaghlul Departs in October 1922 to Join Saad Zaghlul in Exile. Courtesy of Special Collections, J. Willard Marriott Library, University of Utah.

Finally, one cannot be sure, but the equestrian statue here appears to be the same well-known Ibrahim Pasha statue actually located in Ezbekiyya Square. It may be "placed" here near the train station to add a dramatic effect, perhaps to symbolize (for popular appreciation at least) the Wafd's presumed identification with the khedival/sultanic line founded by Muhammad Ali. Such references to the *past* importance of the soon-to-be-royal family may leave one wondering why the figure of the incumbent postwar sultan never appeared in the Wafd posters. Historians of the often-tense relations between the Wafd and the palace (but apparently not with Prince Tusun?) *after* Zaghlul's election victory in 1923–1924 could offer a very likely explanation of that omission.

Only one other poster in the collection is connected to historically symbolic images that would be familiar to popular viewers (here, however, in a completely imaginary "event"). Figure 6.9 shows both Zaghlul and exiled (and self-assigned) Watan Party spokesman Shaykh Shawish on horseback near the Nile riverbanks. The background offers a totally imaginary (and faulty) impression of the opposite shore of the river, placing two famous central Cairo mosques in a specially devised setting meant to guide one's gaze toward the Pyramids of Giza.

There is probably no reason to assume that inclusion here of two very well-known Cairo mosques was meant to deliver an intentional Islamic message beyond pride in what they represent as Egyptian cultural landmarks.[17] In fact, this is one of only two posters in either the JWM/Utah or the LL/Cairo collections in which religious structures of any sort appear. Everything else beyond Zaghlul's standard "Long live the unity of the country" (and especially Shawish's questionable slogan "Long live the leader of the country") is totally imagined by the artist. Moreover, the two

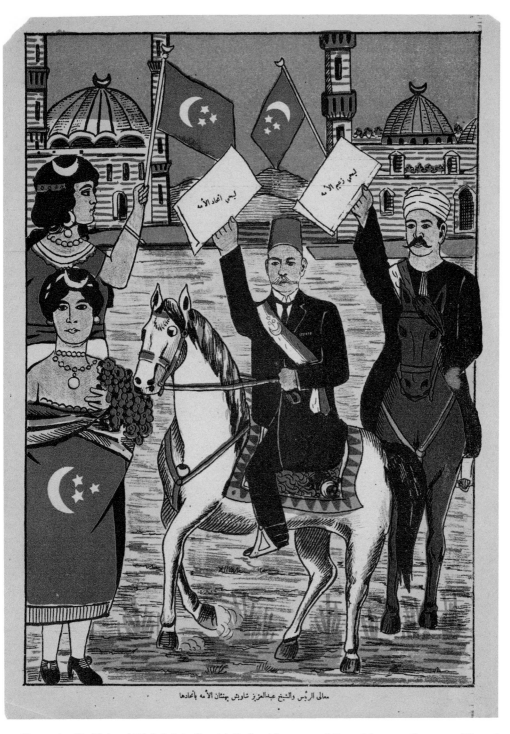

معالي الرئيس والشيخ عبدالعزيز شاويش يهنئان الأمه باتحادها

6.9. Equestrian Zaghlul and ʿAbd al-Aziz Shawish Before Monumental Cairo Mosques. Courtesy of Special Collections, J. Willard Marriott Library, University of Utah.

All Rights Reserved "THE CAIRO PUNCH" Cairo (Egypt)

6.10. Mother Egypt on a Pharaonic Throne. Courtesy of Special Collections, J. Willard Marriott Library, University of Utah.

very famous mosques in the background, for example, are both naïvely placed on the western side of the river, whereas their proper location is in the midst of the historic city east of the Nile.

Possibly the intended aim of this poster, with its symbolic suggestion of a personal political unity that never actually existed, was to convey indirectly a sense of assurance in physical symbols of Egypt's long-enduring identity: the Nile, the Pyramids, and images of its most venerated mosques, all reflecting some form of folk imagery. This may also explain the inclusion (noted here for the first time but repeated frequently in a number of posters that follow) of a celebratory accompanying part of "quasi-pharaonic" maidens to round out the naïve context of folk imagery.

Social Groups in "Passive Unity" around the Raʾîs

One also sees reliance on folk imagery in different posters that, while not commemorating actual historic events, use simple symbolism to allow common folk to imagine themselves as "welcome" in popular circles surrounding Saad Zaghlul. Figure 6.10, for example, done by ʿAbd al-Hamid Zaki's *Cairo Punch* press, offers another example of an imagined Mother Egypt on a pharaonic throne flanked on both sides by Saad and the recurring symbolic figure of Shaykh Shawish.

In the crowd of applauding supporters all but four figures are effendis sporting emblematic tarbushes. In the background to the left are three quite different individuals, one with what appears to be not a typically rural, but tribal headdress and another (with his counterpart in the middle foreground) wearing the typical attire of members of the *ʿulamâʾ* religious class. The third "exceptional"

6.11. Call for Freedom and Independence with Support for Saad and Safiya Zaghlul. Courtesy of Special Collections, J. Willard Marriott Library, University of Utah.

individual—almost directly behind Zaghlul, and the only female in the picture—has a head covering that was apparently becoming increasingly common among well-to-do urban women. The tarbush obstructing a clear view of her face leaves some question (rather easy to answer, if one follows the beginning lines of her face) whether or not she is veiled. Given the somewhat enigmatic image that follows in figure 6.11, however, one can at least wonder whether this is not a totally different and deliberately posed "folk-friendly" representation of Safiya Zaghlul herself.

Figure 6.11, replete with what was clearly by then becoming a repetitive folk version of pharaonic handmaidens, is again identifiable as the work of ʿAbd al-Hamid Zaki, for the first time in association with the lesser-known Egyptian artist, Ahmad al-Shubki. The caption proclaims (in addition to "Freedom" and "Independence") support for both the Raʾîs *and* Safiya Zaghlul, *ar-raʾîsa al-jalîla* ("The Exalted [female] Leader"). Safiya Zaghlul is clad here in a traditional robe (pure white—a style common among the established urban class) and headdress obviously revealing her hair, plus a "stylish," near-transparent veil that actually emphasizes her crimson lips. Such feminine effects, especially the eyes, recall those of the unidentified single woman (who, incidentally, was the only person merely watching, not applauding) in figure 6.10. The contrast with Madame Zaghlul in full Western attire in figure 6.8 could not be greater![18] Figure 6.11 follows the established device of including well-known, but politically "distanced," predecessors from the Watan Party—Mustafa Kamil, Muhammad Farid and, once again, Shaykh Shawish. This trio is supplemented (for the first time?) by the inclusion of a then-sitting Coptic member of the Wafd's higher committee (and future Secretary General of the Wafd during most of the interwar period): William Makram ʿUbayd. With the exception of a quite-distinct series of posters actually

6.12. Egypt in Chains Menaced by British Lion as Egyptian Effendi and Sudanese "Native" Look On. Courtesy of Special Collections, J. Willard Marriott Library, University of Utah.

identifying Egyptian political leaders who would have been poised to run for office in the coming elections in 1923, this appears to be the only preelection poster (at least in the JWM/Utah and LL/Cairo collections) offering an image of one of Zaghlul's actively engaged Wafd associates.[19]

Folk Imagery and the Many Faces of Mother Egypt

Throughout the coming century, there would be a common tendency for caricaturists to combine elements of the Nile Valley's pharaonic heritage and some form of idealized feminine figure to symbolize Egypt.[20] We have already seen an example in the Wafd poster with Mukhtar's famous 1920 statue, Egypt's Awakening (figure 6.4). What is most striking about the Wafd poster artists' presentation of "Mother Egypt" in combination with obvious pharaonic themes is the variation in that idealized and symbolic feminine form. This diversity provides numerous examples of the use of folk imagery in the election campaign posters.

Already, the restrained and docile feminine figure representing Egypt in 'Abd al-Hamid Zaki's *In Memory of Mustafa Kamil* lithograph (figure 5.16) bears no relationship to James Sanua's earlier grim and politically charged use in *Abou Naddara* of a haunting feminine figure exploited

6.13. Dominant Pharaonic Egypt Soothes Caged Lions with Diminutive Sudan, also in Pharaonic Attire. Courtesy of Lesley Lababidy.

by British imperialism.[21] In popularly directed Wafd posters, Mother Egypt often appears in attire and accoutrements that underscore identification with Egypt's pharaonic heritage or, when extremely simple folk images are favored, rather naïve renderings of common Egyptian women.

Most JWM/Utah and LL/Cairo posters containing images of Mother Egypt, whatever the setting, include the stereotypic presence of Saad Zaghlul, either as a participant in different scenes or overseeing the scene from a medallion portrait added to the main drawing. At least two of these complement the imaginary and idealized female figure by adding images of "real" women in a way that may have been intended to symbolize orientations in the Wafd political program.

Figure 6.12 (by an anonymous artist and printer) shows a "semi-pharaonic," jewel-bedecked but manacled Mother Egypt. Her chains are held in the fangs of a lion—a common caricature of the symbolic image of Britain. Standing in the background on a totally flat expanse of sand are dual figures representing close and enthusiastic unity between Egypt (a well-dressed effendi) and a clearly less-sophisticated Sudanese "native." The brief caption reads, "Saad: 'Have patience, O Egypt, for patience is the key to a happy ending.'"

Figure 6.13, which *may* be by Ahmad Za'zû', uses diminutive representations in a different way, allowing Mother Egypt to stroke three small-scale caged lions while a small feminine figure representing the Sudan merely states her name: "Sudan."[22] The three dominant and frequently reappearing personalities beside Zaghlul are each named, with added stereotypic slogans echoing the need for Egypt's independence.

Although figure 6.14 by the *Cairo Punch* press carries similar symbols in its demand for "full independence of the Nile Valley," the artist's vision here is definitely more elaborate in its conception.[23] The simplicity of figure 6.12's use of the "problem" of the imperial lion and 6.13's

All Rights Reserved "THE CAIRO PUNCH" Cairo (Egypt)

مصر والسودان ليحيى الاستقلال التام لوادى النيل

الادارة : رقم ٧ بعيدان اليدق بشارع عبد العزيز بمصر

6.14. Symbolic Unity of the Nile Valley (Duplicate of Figure 1.1).

anthropomorphic representation of the Sudan is replaced in figure 6.14 by two intentionally distinct and magnificent felines meeting below the outstretched and joined arms of idealized Upper and Lower Nile Valley female figures. Both of these women are visibly equal in dignity and impressive stature. Perhaps the *Cairo Punch* artist intended to distance himself from the somewhat belittling representations of the Sudan that appeared almost incidentally in figures 6.12 and 6.13.

A less carefully executed poster (figure 6.15) signed by "A. Ibrahim," includes similar simple exhortations coming from Zaghlul. The Wafd leader is identified here as Ra'îs al-Jîl, (Head, or Leader, of the [new] Generation"). This implies his support for the uniformed young Egyptian boy scout freeing a rather crudely drawn Mother Egypt from her shackles. The image includes one other element of folk imagery that, here and in several following posters, would have been intended to attract the eye of relatively unsophisticated viewers. What better symbol than a caricature of the Sphinx to lend support (with an encouraging paw on the young scout's shoulder) in breaking Egypt's chains?

Figure 6.16 employs even-more simplified symbols. With the Nile and luxuriant vegetation in the background and two miniature pyramids in front, another animated Sphinx declares, "Our hope is in you, Saad." Zaghlul reassures the Sphinx and holds a paper calling for reunification of Egypt and the Sudan. The female image of Egypt here proclaims, "There is no leader but you, Saad," and is clad in heavily decorated robes that do not correspond very clearly to traditional pharaonic styles, especially her Turkish-style babouche footwear.

6.15. Egypt's Chains Broken by Boy Scout. Courtesy of Special Collections, J. Willard Marriott Library, University of Utah.

A similar chain-breaking scene combining a determined, well-attired young effendi with elements of folk imagery appears in figure 6.17. The Nile Valley environment between the Pyramids and Sphinx (both of which are imagined as practically on the river shore) is made quite attractive with river reeds and felucca sailboats. Under the stern medallion portrait of Zaghlul, the Sphinx smiles in approval of the act of breaking Egypt's chains. Here, Mother Egypt is dressed in still another (Arab?) style robe, with only a small detail in the headdress recalling pharaonic symbols.

From Mother Egypt and Supportive Attendants to Popularized Traditional and "Modern" Feminine Figures

The Wafd's efforts to garner support by showing respect for both the rural and urban population, and for Egyptian women in particular, appear in different forms of idealized imagery. Figures 6.18

6.16. "Verbal Support" for Zaghlul from a Talking Sphinx. Courtesy of Special Collections, J. Willard Marriott Library, University of Utah.

and 6.19 by the *Cairo Punch* press, as well as figure 6.20, from the shop of Ahmad Zaʿzûʿ adopt quite original alternative versions of Mother Egypt and representations of women supporting Egypt's call for independence. Figure 6.18, with its intentional symmetry, reemphasizes what appeared, in graphic representations and photographs of the March 1919 Women's March, to be widespread support for the Wafd leadership (here Zaghlul and Prince Tusun) among conservative women in Egypt's main cities. Inclusion of two unveiled women in Western dress and with apparent Western facial features may imply something more than simplistic symmetry on both sides of the main female flag bearer. Symmetry in the positioning of the veiled figures is coupled with representation of identical facial features. It is the caption here that shifts attention from the symbolism of the ever-present, benevolent, onlooking Wafd leaders to the (still rather ambiguous) political aims of women supporting their cause. These aims included women's call for unity between visibly different (but undefined) groups. It states, "Egypt applauds, the gathering together of Egyptian women, and their insistence [lit., "pressing"] for . . . union [between] the races [ʿanâṣir] of the nation."[24]

6.17. Effendi Freeing Egypt Brings Smile to the Sphinx's Face. Courtesy of Special Collections, J. Willard Marriott Library, University of Utah.

6.18. Egyptian Women Call for Union Between the Races/Ethnicities ('Anâṣir) of the Nation. Courtesy of Lesley Lababidy.

In figure 6.19, by Zaki and the *Cairo Punch*, both the style of raiment and Egypt's crown decorated with precious stones suggest another image of Egypt as a woman. Her figure beside traditionally dressed urban women—plus the presumably egalitarian symbol of boy *and* girl Egyptian scouts—is not that different from previous symbolic representations. But lack of any written slogan might have created something of a quandary for viewers unacquainted with the newly founded international scout movement.[25]

Za'zû''s image of Egyptian women in figure 6.20 is again quite different and particularly striking. It "admits" only one man (the violinist in the three-member musical group) in the midst of the most-diversified and overall most-representative group of women supporters of the Wafd among all the posters in the JWM/Utah collection.

In figure 6.20, while all but two "symbolic" women in Western attire in the *Cairo Punch* lithograph wear veils (again, near transparent) and dark vestments to signify traditional modesty, only one out of the sixteen women in the entourage of Mother Egypt is prominently and completely veiled. Overall, however, this poster stands out for its frank visual celebration of Egyptian womanhood and femininity. Simple natural beauty is communicated in a variety of facial features. There is a clear diversity of female types in the scene, yet all appear to be equally proud of their individual identities. Unlike almost "declarative" representations of Westernized women (particularly in the commemorative event pictures cited earlier, figures 6.7 and 6.8, for example), there is no effort here to imply that removal of facial veils involves a symbolic decision to identify with

All Rights Reserved "THE CAIRO PUNCH" Cairo (Egypt)

مصر : عليكم بالاتحاد يا بناتي الاعزاء، فهو الذي يبلغكم الآمال

(كلية الشرق عنوانة لجريدة السياسة للصورة عدد ٢٠٥)

6.19. Regal Feminine Figure of Egypt Accompanied by Boy and Girl Scouts. Courtesy of Special Collections, J. Willard Marriott Library, University of Utah.

one section of a changing local culture or another. The women pictured here (even in the case of the completely veiled individual) are natural and relaxed in their appearance, whether they represent urban or rural cultural traditions.

Although Za'zû' obviously placed Zaghlul's image and the accustomed symbols of Egyptian flags in this scene (even on the peasant woman's water jug, labeled *bahr al-Nîl* (literally, the "Sea of the Nile," an Egyptian term for the Nile River), there is no other political slogan. This suggests that the diverse assemblage supports the Wafd through the simple fact of their daily lives, without any need for open political declarations. It is also worth noting that, unlike the "anonymous" representations of traditionally veiled women in figure 6.18, there is an effort here to portray individual facial features.

Figure 6.21, probably printed sometime later by the *Cairo Punch* press, is a very different form of contrast (though still implying mutual respect) for and between Egyptian women from the "countryside" on the one hand, and those adopting more "modern" styles of the city on the other. As a political poster, the shared cause of the Wafd, however diminutive in the small card with Saad's portrait, plus the simple phrases "Long live free Egypt," and "Egypt and its cherished one (*habîbuhâ*, i.e., Zaghlul)," serve the symbolic function of placing the two different women on common ground. Stylistically, it seems clear that the artist intended both figures to represent and compliment feminine finesse in their equally elegant clothing and headwear, as well as their proud demeanor.

6.20. Broad Representation of Egyptian Women with Mixed-Gender Musical Group. Courtesy of Special Collections, J. Willard Marriott Library, University of Utah.

Winnowing before the Elections: Identification of Leading Candidates in 1923

Almost all the popular Wafd campaign posters reviewed up to this point contain various facets of folk imagery—a method clearly designed to attract the attention of viewers with only a very general idea of what Egypt's first parliamentary elections might entail. When it came to more-informed potential voters concerning the actual personalities who were devoted to organizing the Wafd program, however, the same lithographers seem to have followed a different tack. Although they continued to rely on fairly simplistic symbolism, depictions of assumed active organizers of the movement tended to omit all but the most basic hints of folk imagery. As signs of possible disagreement (at the executive level at least) over the Raʾis's leadership methods grew, the apparent importance of identifying individual Wafd supporters seems to have given rise to a closing ring of "realistic" political choices.

The review of the first period of Wafd politics in chapters 1 and 2 described early signs of division among the first Egyptians (most already well-established) who initially supported Saad Zaghlul's leadership. Differences began as early as the Raʾis's first bid to deal with British High Commissioner Wingate in the last months of 1918. They became more pronounced as nationalist demands grew more complex, and Zaghlul's earliest associates began to sense that their own political future might be better served by distancing themselves from his leadership. This even led some who had supported him to pose their candidature in his absence for offices that could run counter to the Raʾis's preferred strategy. The last group of original campaign posters reviewed here may well contain hints of such shifts in loyalty leading up to the 1923 elections. As such, they

6.21. Elegant Urban and Rural Feminine Figures Support Egypt and Its "Cherished One" (ḥabîbuhâ). Courtesy of Special Collections, J. Willard Marriott Library, University of Utah.

offer partial, here graphic, documentation of the leadership "selection" process noted in many studies of early Wafd party history.[26]

One individual who would eventually be the focus of one of the most spectacular of these fallings out (albeit long after Zaghlul's demise) should be noted here. Coptic Christian William Makram ʿUbayd was perhaps the first *actual*, as opposed to symbolic political activist to be pictured in close association with the Raʾîs in a poster reproduced earlier in this chapter (figure 6.1). ʿUbayd would eventually serve as the secretary general of the party, ceding the main party leadership (and several appointments to the prime ministership) to Zaghlul's immediate successor in 1927, Mustafa Nahhas. Both men merit particular mention as we examine these last few posters because they came to reflect, by the end of the campaign process, *visible* evidence of a winnowing process carried out by the Raʾîs.

Several posters suggest that perhaps only three among the (at least visibly) most-important early Wafd leaders would pass the internal selection process allowing them to claim public recognition as potential candidates by the time of the 1923 elections. Apparently only one of these, however (ʿUbayd), was well enough known among popular observers to have his image regularly included as part of the consciously crafted propaganda posters dominated from the outset by the Raʾîs's patronizing presence. This reinforces the earlier suggestion that poster artists must have been encouraged (required?) to limit figures for inclusion alongside Zaghlul to persons well enough known to help the Wafd through repeated symbolic, not necessarily practical working relationships. This was obviously the case of Shaykh Shawish, Muhammad Farid, and Prince Tusun from the outset. The Wafd may have used their images conveniently "from afar" up to the 1922–1923 campaign but seems to have eliminated them once the question of actual parliamentary candidacy approached.

6.22. Members of the Egyptian Delegation to the General Peace Conference in Paris (in Arabic). Courtesy of Special Collections, J. Willard Marriott Library, University of Utah.

Only in stages did printers depart from elementary symbolism and colorful folk imagery to print posters bearing the names and faces of relatively little-known but apparently influential Wafd supporters for general distribution. This is the case in a poster (figure 6.22, possibly the earliest in the JWM/Utah collection) done at the time Zaghlul's first "expanded" delegation received authorization to travel to Europe with hopes of participating in the upcoming postwar peace conference. This poster seeks to provide names and *photographic* portraits of all the expanded delegation members.[27] Still, the printer took care to incorporate symbolic content that became characteristic of the hand-drawn graphics between 1920 and 1923: a portrait photo and an elaborate poetic tribute (delivered by the female pharaonic figure at his side?) to deceased Watan Party founder, Mustafa Kamil.

Given the large number of individuals chosen for the delegation, one can assume considerable variation among them in terms of their influence with Zaghlul. Only a few—perhaps five pictured in the poster—had already attained recognition as intellectual or wealthy leaders in Egyptian society and were destined for significant roles in Egyptian politics in the ensuing decades, though not necessarily as Wafdists. Four out of the total group were Copts, reflecting the Wafd's pledge to include Egypt's minority Christian population in its popular bid for independence.[28]

It is worth noting here that several of the best-known individuals would abandon Wafdist leadership ranks either just before or shortly after the 1923 elections. (This includes four of Zaghlul's most-notable early collaborators, Ahmad Lutfi al-Sayyid, Muhammad Mahmud, 'Ali Shaarawi, and Isma'il Sidqi—all pictured as part of the 1919 delegation.) While lesser-known personalities in the fourteen-member group are more difficult to trace, we shall see, or at least suggest, that only six of Saad's earliest supporters pictured in this poster (Mustafa Nahhas, Hamid al-Basil Pasha, Muhammad Mahmud Pasha, Muhammad 'Ali Bey, 'Abd al-Latif al-Makabati Bey, and Sinut Hanna Bey) survived the political selection process that thinned Wafd central leadership ranks in just a few years.[29] This process, though not openly publicized, may have affected choices as to who would appear alongside the Ra'is in the posters printed stage by stage as the actual legislative elections of 1923 approached.

The next poster, figure 6.23, *Heroes of Freedom*, suggests that Wafd poster printers would be reattuned to the "thinning process," placing one, then another, of Zaghlul's close associates either in or out of the limelight according to changing political winds.

After including the still "required" but essentially symbolic portraits of Mustafa Kamil and the by-then deceased Muhammad Farid, figure 6.23 shows only three individuals who traveled to Europe in the original Delegation of Fourteen, joined by the first two postwar prime ministers, Husayn Rushdi and 'Adli Yakin.[30] During the interim period when Zaghlul was having difficulty convincing his followers to recognize his political dominance both within the European delegation and at home, these last two rather overtly considered making bids of their own to attract shifting loyalties to themselves.[31] Once that point of apparent compromise was passed, neither Rushdi nor Yakin appeared again in graphics alongside Zaghlul. At least that is the impression one gains from the (chronologically) last poster in the JWM/Utah collection.

If figure 6.22 depicting the original Wafd delegation poised to leave for Europe in 1919 is the earliest surviving poster in the Marriott Library collection, figure 6.24 is probably the latest. It offers last-minute advertisements for candidates who were, by 1923, widely recognized among Zaghlul's closest associates. Indeed, several were ready, as events would show, to participate as members of his first cabinet following the Wafd's election success at the end of the year.

At this date in 1923, the artist here could dispense with any further need to suggest joint sponsorship from contemporary politicians who might try to challenge Zaghlul's leadership, the apparent but unsuccessful cases of Rushdi and Yakin. The poster also leaves out any further

أبطال   الحرية

محمد باشا محمود   اسماعيل باشا صدقي

عبد باشا يكن   حسين باشا رشدي

صاحب المعالي رئيسنا المحبوب
﴿ سعد باشا زغلول ﴾

تطلب من شركة رحمدبس
للحفر والزنكوغراف
بشارع الرويبي نمرة ٣ بمصر

6.23. The Heroes of Freedom. Courtesy of Special Collections, J. Willard Marriott Library, University of Utah.

reference at all to the three personalities who, without ever actually participating in the Wafd's formative stages, had lent "symbolic" support in many earlier political caricatures: Mustafa Kamil, Muhammad Farid, and Shaykh Shawish. Instead, two individuals were pictured—Mustafa al-Nahhas and one of Zaghlul's own nephews, Fathallah Pasha Barakat, who would be appointees to ministerial positions in Zaghlul's first cabinet.[32] A third person here, Makram 'Ubayd, would, as stated above, remain a leader of the Wafd for almost two decades. Equally important, this image documents the fact that both Muhammad Mahmud Pasha and Hamid al-Basil Pasha, were the *only* original Wafdist leaders to figure among Zaghlul's close confidents *in all three* of these selected posters leading up to the 1923 election. The other four individuals, 'Atif Barakat Bey (brother of soon-to-be minister Fathallah Barakat, and Zaghlul's youngest nephew),

6.24. The Closing Circle Around Zaghlul by 1922–1923. Courtesy of Special Collections, J. Willard Marriott Library, University of Utah.

Sinut Hanna Bey, ʿAbd al-Latif al-Makabati Bey, and Muhammad ʿAli Bey, had all been among the original fourteen Paris delegates in 1919. As such, they were assumed to be working closely together for the same political goals defined by Zaghlul, the Raʾîs. It is apparent from contemporary sources described in the Conclusion, however, that skeptics of the presumed "unity" of politicians pictured here around Zaghlul were prepared to counter posters such as figure 6.24 with satirical, even very biting, newspaper graphics of their own.

Whatever other biographical peculiarities one might extract from this graphic record of the Wafd's leadership ranks just before it won its first parliamentary majority, figure 6.24 still contains at least one symbol again suggesting a "'reality' behind a public figure . . . designed . . . [although through some form of distortion] to influence the spectator." For example, the caricature portrait of Hamid al-Basil Pasha (always placed top center, always in a traditional robe, and without tarbush in all three posters reproduced here) is prominently depicted in robes and headwear emblematic of his native province of Fayyum and his family's bedouin heritage. Perhaps the printer who did this last original poster may have wanted to assure voters that the Wafd sought to be a reflection of all symbols recognized by the Egyptian population as a whole and from all regions and social backgrounds.

By the end of the period covered by the Wafd's election poster campaign, then, there are some remaining traces of the use of symbolism and some folk imagery. The images in the JWM/Utah and LL/Cairo collections, however, are still a long way from any implication that satire or humor could conceivably have a place in the political caricatures used to garner support for the Wafd.

Equally distant from the idealized images offered by pro-Wafd lithographers in the small printing shops that produced these posters was another trend just beginning to affect the place of caricature art in Egypt: the arrival of popular journalistic illustrations. In fairly short time, these would reduce the product of shops such as those of the Nationalist Illustrations partners to near obsolescence. Not only would popular journalists and caricaturists thrive on the use of satire and humor, but they would not hesitate to provide graphic hints that—even among Zaghlul's closest associates and including several figures pictured side by side in figure 6.24—political infighting had already begun in the very shadow of the Raʾîs.

CONCLUSION

Evolving Stages of Caricature by the Mid–1920s:
Sophisticated Satirical Comics and Daily Imagery

Without research that extends beyond the scope of this book, it would be difficult to know when, and under what circumstances, works by Egyptian political caricaturists became recognized as major prototypes in the Arabic speaking world. Ultimately such developments would include, as Professor Afaf Marsot suggests, integration of the *nukta*—a typically Egyptian form of humor—as part of caricaturists' mode of incorporating political messages into their work. Whatever happened, the prominent graphic style of works produced by small-scale lithograph printers supporting the Wafd in the 1922–1923 election campaign was left behind—and in relatively short order.

Different forms of caricature with political themes did indeed appear in Egyptian newspapers as early as the mid-1920s. These continued into the 1930s and certainly in the decades beyond.[1] All stand in contrast to the rather elementary Wafd political posters conceived and executed just after World War I by small printing shops.

New features emerging under clearly changed sociopolitical conditions no longer emphasized simple "folk imagery" but turned toward a humorous (albeit discomforting, *not* comforting) panorama of situations with images of daily Egyptian life and politics.[2] Part of the changed sociopolitical conditions that made this new direction possible was the remarkable expansion of the role of the daily press in the lives of almost all classes of Egyptians, not only the most educated, in the second half of the twentieth century.

Professor Marsot's 1971 suggestion is generally true that, in the earlier interwar period, "the popular press tried to cater to . . . an audience which included the intelligentsia as well as the man in the street, [by offering] articles of a lighter vein . . . [and thus] the cartoon appeared."[3] Any commentator would have to recognize, however, that the process took decades to produce the "full *nukta*," one that delivered a direct, humorous appeal while implying subtle, not necessarily humorous political messages.

Indications of new forms of political caricature in the recently introduced popular Egyptian press appeared already by the end of the Protectorate in 1922 and the period immediately before Egypt's first parliamentary election in 1923. Not surprisingly, the artists who drew these caricatures frequently focused on the highly publicized prime minister of Egypt's first popularly elected parliament, Saad Zaghlul, and the political party he founded. Their visions definitely contrasted with the privately printed election campaign images that presented him in stern but ideal terms, surrounded by symbols embodied by past or contemporary personalities or by scenes meant to communicate "comforting" popular folk images.

Probably the best-known early illustrated publications in Egypt that help trace this process are *al-Laṭâ'if al-muṣawwara* ("Illustrated Tidbits," or "Subtleties," hereafter *al-Lataif*) and *al-Kashkûl* ("the Scrapbook," hereafter *al-Kashkul*). In addition to the much better-known *Ruz al-Yusuf*, both are mentioned extensively in Beth Baron's *Egypt as a Woman,* but only in a few other studies dealing with the early post–World War I stages of Egyptian political caricature art.[4] What is striking, however, is the fact that *none* of these studies seem to have been aware of how close in time, if not at all in spirit, these postwar caricatures were to the examples of "folk imagery" that appeared in Egypt during the few previous years as the Wafd Party organized itself for the elections of 1923–1924.

Periodicals like *al-Lataif* frequently used simple drawings to accompany articles containing only a minimum of detailed political content. A general reference source suggests that *al-Lataif* provided an "easy to read text," while encouraging readers "to submit . . . photographs of unusual occurrences, crimes, sporting events, celebrities . . . , as well as political cartoons or caricatures."[5] Although caricatures printed in such illustrated journals did contain elements of satire not seen in Egypt since well before World War I, they clearly did not offer anything resembling the typically light-hearted Egyptian *nukat* (pl.), or "jokes" that became so common in later years.

The earliest examples of *al-Lataif*'s politically motivated caricature drawings I was able to locate appear in ʿAbdullah al-Nâʿîm's *Ḥikâyât fi'l-fakâhati wa'l-kârîkâtîr*, plus a number in Beth Baron's monograph *Egypt as a Woman.* There are also extensive reproductions of early caricatures from *al-Kashkul* (and several early examples from *al-Lataif* in a 1997 master's thesis completed at the American University in Cairo.[6]

Early politically oriented caricatures selected by Baron come mainly from *al-Lataif*'s contemporary, and apparently rival, illustrated newspaper, *al-Kashkul.* These related mainly to politics of the day, and Baron's choices tend to reflect her own focus on female representations either symbolizing "The Egyptian Nation" or depicting women who were identifiable because of their public political activities.[7] But an additional distinguishing factor characterizing the two illustrated papers must be kept in mind. Because of *al-Lataif*'s pro-Wafd reputation, Baron's view of *al-Kashkul* as a politically motivated "counter-movement" places its divergent approach to political caricature and the "not so revered" persona of Saad Zaghlul in clearer perspective. The only other source offering enough specific examples to emphasize this essential detail is Tonia Rifaey's 1997 master's thesis.[8] Very notable among these were several that mocked interpersonal rivalries between Wafdists generally portrayed as completely devoted to Zaghlul's leadership— at least according to the Wafd posters reproduced in chapter 6.

Figure 7.1, dated August 24, 1923, proclaims (as Hamid al-Basil and Fathallah Barakat attack one another viciously and an undisturbed Zaghlul looks on), "It's you or me, you know, not the both of us [who will lead]." Another, even less discreet hint of infighting, appears in a caricature

رابطة الوفد سعد محمد باشا الباسل وفتحالله باشا بركات

يا ... يا محرشي جمرك . انت بدل بوليس بتمزقني . . .

7.1. Violent Struggle Between Wafdists Hamid al-Basil and Fathallah Barakat. Reproduced by permission from Tonia Rifaey.

سينور حنا ـ لا حياة للوفد لا زوال هذه الرؤوس فهو يقدمها لكم ويوصيكم تهشها جيداً . لأنها دسمة أن سوس هضمها عسير هضمي

7.2. Removing Heads of Wafdist Rivals. Reproduced by permission from Tonia Rifaey.

7.3. Zaghlul "Imposes" his Representation on the Backward Sudan. Reproduced by permission from Tonia Rifaey.

of Sinut Hanna carrying the bloody heads of four identifiable colleagues (including Mustafa Nahhas), that states, "There is no life for the Wafd without removal of these heads" (figure 7.2).[9]

After the Wafd won the 1923–1924 elections, *al-Kashkul* also published drawings that were strongly critical of Zaghlul's political dealings. Almost all provide signs of the reemergence of caricatural satire and iconoclasm that would put the Wafd's earlier reliance on folk imagery to definitive rest. One illustration (in this case fairly "easy going") depicts Zaghlul deigning to instruct (in a classroom decorated by his portrait wearing a very sporty Western-style hat) the new Wafd majority parliament of inexperienced "rural notables . . . dressed in *gallabiyya* and turban[s]."[10] One of the latter holds an elementary school manual reading "*âlif, bâ, tâ*" (initial Arabic letters "a, b, t").

Another satirical (but hardly "humorous") *al-Kashkul* caricature from December 14, 1923, shows the Ra'îs with a Sudanese in primitive tribal dress overlooking the still-empty national assembly hall (figure 7.3). The Sudanese claims that Sudan had twelve seats in the (abortive 'Urabist nationalist-dominated) 1882 Assembly, but it would have *none* in 1924. Zaghlul retorts, "As long as I am in the parliament, I represent you and everyone else."[11]

One sees a different approach to political caricature in the pages of *al-Lataif*—clearly a defender of the Wafd. Its satirical critique of the political dilemmas faced by the Wafd before, during, and after Zaghlul's first and second tenures as prime minister would be numerous.

Once Zaghlul took up the prime minister's job after 1923, rising problems of internal politics between Egyptians themselves provided material for countering critics' denunciation of the Wafd's early failures, particularly its bid to remove the Four Reserved Points that Britain had left behind when it ended the Protectorate. In *The Road [to] the Negotiations* (figure 7.4), a highly

7.4. The Road to the Negotiations. Image in the public domain.

caricatured female figure labeled "the Egyptian people" (no longer a simple folk image of Mother Egypt) in a stalled automobile calling out to Zaghlul, "You promised me you would take me to the negotiations, so what happened?" Zaghlul answers, "Yes, and my promise still holds, but the petrol [in the figurative sense here] is defective (colloquial Egyptian *malakhbaṭ*)." In the background, two local "resisters," or opponents, congratulate themselves on causing the "fuel problem" that was blocking the Wafd's goals.[12]

The same type of caricature appeared in *al-Lataif*'s denunciation of "plotting" by well-known Egyptian political personalities. Some of these, after earlier, unquestioned alignment with the Ra'is, found themselves under suspicion once the Wafd was in power. Such was the case of Huda Shaarawi, wife of one of Zaghlul's most prominent early backers, and herself very well known as president of the Wafd Women's Central Committee. When she became personally compromised in a court case pitting *al-Kashkul* against Zaghlul, she was reprimanded and forced to resign her leadership post. In figure 7.5, Zaghlul uses word play on her name (*huda*, or "right path") to mock her taking the "*wrong*" path. It shows Huda Shaarawi's weight on the "scale of truth" as "very heavy." Beside her, the mustachioed human head on a performing circus dog probably represents *al-Kashkul*'s publisher and Wafd critic, Sulayman Fawzi.[13]

The style in these few selected examples suggests essential differences between the intended reading audience of Egypt's popular political press in the mid-1920s and the much simpler aims served by graphics used in the Wafd's initial electoral campaign. Provenance of the latter, I have argued, grew out of a slowly evolving tradition of "folk imagery" that could not assume extensive knowledge of current events on the part of viewers. Anything pictured could be immediately appreciated for its reflection of commonly shared values.

7.5. The Scale of Truth. Image in the public domain.

فبراير ١٩٥٣

« تناقش لجنة الدستور غدا النظام الجمهوري »

المواطن المصري ــ ده رقبته انقطعت قبل القطر ما يفوت عليه !!

7.6. The Imminent Demise of Constitutional Monarchy (February 1953). Image in the public domain.

What one sees in caricatures published in Egypt's popular press by the mid-1920s, on the other hand, is a reflection of artists' responses to the changing nature of their audience, as parliamentary politics became more complicated. That audience, like very distant readers of European or American publications such as *Punch* or *The New Yorker*, had to be abreast of what was happening, not only in the political sphere, but at various levels of their own society.

Once local political debates over responsibilities of governance in Egypt ceased to be simple, it was no longer possible to portray political actors in black-and-white terms. This began to create a situation, again something characteristic of satirical publications like *Punch*, in which any and all parties could be vulnerable to criticism for their shortcomings. In the concluding examples of Egyptian caricature art offered here, the satirical spotlight is increasingly turned inward, less as a sign of blanket approval or denunciation of an obvious opponent but something more akin to almost-painful self-critique. Hence, the coming phases of Egyptian twentieth-century political caricature would emphasize satirical humor even in less than humorous situations. The rising generations of caricaturists would include such outstanding examples as 'Abd al-Moneim Rakha (1911–1989), 'Abd al-Sami (1916–1985), and Salah Jahin (1930–1986) and others. Such considerations may have led to El Hakk's and Alleaume's choice of title for their book reviewing cartoons from the 1980s Egyptian press: *Essayons d'en rire*, or *Let's Try to Laugh about It*.

I take a cautious risk in suggesting the following conclusion, which may go against opinions held by specialists in interwar or post-1945 Egyptian caricature art. Beginning with the generation of artists like 'Abd al-Sami (1916–1985), Egyptian cartoons may in some sense be said to have come to reflect caricatural traditions that are almost universal. There were, obviously, still-important differences in cultural content between 'Abd al-Sami and his Egyptian peers and the innumerable contemporary political caricaturists in Europe or America. But, in both cases, one can begin to assume that even before the advent of the internet, persons informed of events around the world via the press could begin to understand "daily imagery" from various caricatural sources.

The last Egyptian caricature I have chosen here, however (by 'Abd al-Sami, February, 1953), showing Masri Effendi (the iconic "Mister Egypt"), watching a train about to roll over King Faruq and Egypt's thirty-one-year-old constitutional monarchy (and with it the *original* Wafd party, outlawed some months before), can be fairly easily understood, even without translation of the subcaption.[14]

The same could *not* be said of the political campaign caricatures supporting the Wafd movement in the immediate post–World War I years—at least if one retains the assumption that Egyptian "folk imagery" required inbred values of Egyptian folk culture. This concluding remark applies quite well, for example, to figure 6.9. Despite all their outward simplicity, such caricatures still require a degree of folk-cultural background to be understood, not necessarily awareness of "daily imagery."

Preface

1. To distinguish reproductions of originals from the two collections that appear in this book, the abbreviation JWM/Utah will be used to refer to Marriott Library holdings. The abbreviation LL/Cairo identifies items from the Lesley Lababidi collection.

2. The Arabic word *wafd,* "delegation," is part of the full name *al-wafd al-miṣrî* (the Egyptian Delegation) adopted by the small group of individuals who claimed the task of representing Egypt (then a British Protectorate) in the post–World War I peace talks in Europe. The name was carried forward by the political party that was active in Egypt between 1919 and its dissolution in 1952. A large number of general histories of modern Egypt deal with the early activities of the Wafd. Publications in Arabic are too numerous to list here. Perhaps the earliest, printed in Cairo in 1921 by Mahmud Abu al-Fath under the title *al-Masʾala al-miṣriyah waʾl-wafd* (*The Egyptian question and the Wafd*), does not list the publisher. A very lengthy study by Jamal Badawi, *Tarîkh al-wafd* (*History of the Wafd*) was published in Cairo in 2003 by Dâr al-Shurûq. Accounts that fit the general needs of this project are available (among others) in two older but widely recognized works in English: Janice J. Terry, *The Wafd: 1919–1952* (London: Third World Center, 1982), and Marius Deeb, *Party Politics in Egypt: The Wafd and Its Rivals, 1919–1939* (London: Ithaca Press, 1979). A more recent and concise section on the Wafd's early postwar activity is in Ziad Fahmy, *Ordinary Egyptians: Creating the Modern Nation through Popular Culture* (Palo Alto, CA: Stanford University Press, 2011, 136–153).

3. Art historians offer, of course, many definitions of folk art. Most inevitably return to the supposition that folk art is the product of (usually) anonymous amateurs whose work reflects commonplace subjects drawn from the artists' own cultural milieu. Some though not all of the lithographs appearing in this book could qualify as folk art, but I have preferred to use the term "folk imagery" when describing a fairly wide variety of selected materials. Although the content in many illustrations to be discussed was chosen from commonplace surroundings and did represent the local cultural milieu depicted, the artists made a more or less conscious decision to include such familiar images in their work. This would have been done to achieve some communicative goal that, even in elementary political contexts, could qualify such images as propaganda, not in the widely used "activist" sense, but because they were done with a particular intention.

4. Afaf Lutfi al-Sayyid Marsot, "The Cartoon in Egypt," *Studies in Comparative Society and History* 13, no. 1 (1971):2–15.

5. Ibid., 2.

6. Near the end of his career, Dr. Atiya's crowning contribution to the scholarly world was the publication, in eight volumes, of the *The Coptic Encyclopedia* (New York: Macmillan, 1991). The final sections were completed posthumously by his wife, the late Lola Atiya.

7. The Middle East Library holds Dr. Atiya's own private papers plus the papers of Dr. Martin Levey (1913–1970), who worked throughout his career as a chemist and historian of science on original manuscripts in the fields of medieval Arabic medicine and pharmacology. Other collections include the private papers of Ahmad Zaki Abu Shadi (d. 1955), internationally known Egyptian poet and founder of the *Apollo* literary journal, and the papers of Dr. Fayez Sayegh (1922–1980), noted Arab educator and United Nations diplomat.

8. Dr. Atiya mentioned his participation as a student in the popular demonstrations that followed World War I to Professor Donald Reid when the latter interviewed him in 1986.

9. Harvard's Advanced Leadership Initiative Program was initially conceived as an innovative "third stage in higher education." It sought to explore ways to engage people of diverse nationalities and professional experience in a "think tank" to address issues relating to poverty, global health, the environment, and education.

10. Marilyn Booth's 2013 study of *al-Siyâsah al-muṣawwara*, (hereafter cited using its English title, the *Cairo Punch*), "What Is in a Name? Branding *Punch* in Cairo," is in Hans Harder and Barbara Mittler, editors, *Asian Punches: A Transcultural Affair* (New York: Springer, 2013), 271–303.

Chapter 1

1. For a review of the post–World War I League of Nations settlements envisioned by the abortive 1920 Treaty of Sèvres and its successor, the 1923 Treaty of Lausanne, see Briton Cooper Busch, *Mudros to Lausanne: Britain's Frontier in West Asia, 1918–1923* (Albany: State University of New York Press, 1976). Original texts of the two "Turkish" treaties are in Lawrence Martin, *The Treaties of Peace, 1919–1923* (New York: Carnegie Endowment for International Peace, 1924).

2. On Muhammad ʿAli's rise and consolidation of power as Egypt's governor until his death in 1848, see, among others, Afaf Lutfi al-Sayyid-Marsot, *Egypt in the Reign of Muhammad Ali* (Cambridge: Cambridge University Press, 1984). A more recent monograph is by Khaled Fahmy, *Mehmed Ali: From Ottoman Governor to Ruler of Egypt* (London: Oneworld, 2009). In some cases, "compact" background information is available and sufficient in general reference publications, for example, in Philip Mattar, general editor, *The Encyclopedia of the Middle*

East and North Africa (Detroit: MacMillan, 2nd ed., 2005), these will be cited rather than full monographic studies.

3. A classic account of these eventually disastrous financial dealings was written by David Landes, *Bankers and Pashas: International Finance and Economic Imperialism in Egypt* (Cambridge: Harvard University Press, 1958). See also Byron Cannon, *Politics of Law and the Courts in Nineteenth-Century Egypt* [hereafter *Politics of Law*] (Salt Lake City: University of Utah Press, 1988).

4. Ibid., 54–61. Capitulatory status refers to the existence of "treaties of friendship and commerce" signed between the Ottoman Empire and, eventually, most major Western governments. These defined various extraterritorial privileges for nationals of all signatory parties, many affecting conditions of trade and court jurisdiction.

5. This controversial event was considered by some to be a move by Disraeli to assure Britain's control over the "lifeline" that connected it with its imperial sphere in India. (See the near-contemporary satirical caricature from *Punch*, reproduced as figure 3.5).

6. Cannon, *Politics of Law*, chapter 5.

7. Accounts of the emerging effendi "class" in the Middle East offer various definitions of the term. Generally speaking, in the latter stages of the Ottoman period, it was applied to individuals who, because of their educational background and adoption of various styles (in dress, mode of daily and home life) no longer observed all aspects of traditional culture, tending toward "Western" modes. See, for example, the following extract from Lucie Ryzova, *L'Effendiyya, ou la modernité contestée* (Cairo: CEDEJ, 2004), 23–24 (translation from the French by the present author): "After being associated with Ottoman high bureaucratic level appointments . . . at the end of the nineteenth century . . . the profile of *affandiyya* status changed considerably. First with the emergence of new trades and new institutes, the term . . . ceased being associated with the state bureaucracy. It began to represent . . . a new "cognitive universe": the new urban society with new social institutions and new lifestyles. The effendi is not just a . . . bureaucrat; he is distinguished above all by his education and [level of] culture." An alternative description of the *affandiyya* appears in Ziad Fahmi, *Ordinary Egyptians*, 23–24: "[Many new students] entered the growing school system to feed the emerging

[bureaucracy]. Graduates . . . would . . . fill the ranks of the . . . *affandiyya* class. [These] were literate Egyptian urbanites who often wore *tarabish*; they donned Western style clothes and typically worked in the civil service and in the [legal, medical] 'free professions.'"

8. Even when a change of government in Britain in 1885 led to a conservative government's willingness to negotiate terms with Istanbul for ending the occupation (known to historians as the Drummond-Wolff Convention), foreign rivals refused to cooperate, clinging to the capitulatory status quo.

9. Roger Owen's biography of Lord Cromer, *Lord Cromer: Victorian Imperialist, Edwardian Proconsul* (Oxford: Oxford University Press, 2004), 117–349, provides an extensive account of Cromer's long tenure in Egypt until 1907. Owen's scholarship helped offset many, often quite biased, writings cited by generations of historians. Foremost among biased accounts, of course, was Cromer's own *Modern Egypt* (New York: Macmillan, 1908).

10. The biographical backgrounds of each of these important late-nineteenth-century Egyptian social and political elites are, of course, quite complex. Brief mention of Muhammad Pasha Sharif here might lead the curious reader to an article based on selected private papers held by Sharif's descendants: Byron Cannon, "Transferts de valeurs de pairs aux proches: la correspondance familiale de Muhammad Pacha Chérif, 1860–1882," in Alain Roussillon, editor, *Entre réforme sociale et movement national* (Cairo: CEDEJ, 1995), 163–179.

11. The lithograph from the private LL/Cairo collection reproduced in the Preface and discussed as figure 6.14 in chapter 6 is a striking example of this graphic linkage.

12. On the *ahliyya* court system, see Cannon, *Politics of Law*, especially chapter 7.

13. Abbas would "merit" an entire critical memoir from the pen of Baring (then Lord Cromer) in 1915: *Abbas II* (London: Macmillan, 1915).

14. On Fahmi's key role into the first decades of the twentieth century, including the marriage of his daughter to Saad Zaghlul, see chapter 2, note 3.

15. On these events and establishment of the Anglo-Egyptian Condominium, see Philip Mattar, general editor, *The Encyclopedia of the Middle East and North Africa*, vol. 1, 2nd ed. (Detroit: Thomson Gale, 2004), 518, 629.

16. According to the Entente Cordiale of 1904, France agreed to recognize Britain's preferred position in Egypt in return for British recognition of France's growing interests in the Kingdom of Morocco—interests that led to a French protectorate in Morocco in 1912.

17. See chapter 4, figure 4.6.

18. These first references to Shaykh 'Abd al-'Aziz Shawish, who will appear repeatedly when the discussion turns to the Wafd political posters, adopt the most common transliterated spelling of his surname. In some cases, authors have transcribed the name as al-Jawish.

19. See Archie Hunter, *Power and Passion in Egypt: A Life of Sir Eldon Gorst, 1861–1911* (London: I. B. Tauris, 2007).

20. The major landmark of Kitchener's career came not in this period in Egypt, however, but when he was appointed Secretary of State for War at the outbreak of World War I. He died while in that office in a naval catastrophe in 1916.

21. On *al-Jarîda* and the Hizb al-Umma, see Afaf Marsot, *Egypt's Liberal Experiment* (Berkeley: University of California Press, 1977), 222.

Chapter 2

1. Some accounts suggest, without actual documentation, that since *al-Waqâ'i'* was edited by Shaykh Muhammad 'Abduh in this period, young Zaghlul may have come under 'Abduh's influence during his work with the official gazette. Any real chance of 'Abduh having such an effect would, however, probably have come later, when 'Abduh's reputation as an outstanding figure in Egyptian intellectual (and cultural reform) circles was firmly established. In any event, an indirect suggestion of 'Abduh's presumed support for the principles announced by the Wafd would appear (years after his death) in at least one of the post-1918 posters.

2. Kamil may have begun seeking support from sympathetic foreigners opposed to the British presence in Egypt, especially French, when he studied law in Toulouse. The Anglo-Egyptian campaign to reenter the Sudan occurred in that same period, providing him with a French audience anxious to hear his denunciation of Britain's move to strengthen its Egyptian presence at France's expense. A valuable source documenting Kamil's French connection was edited by Kamil's brother 'Ali Kamil, *Egyptian-French Letters Addressed to Mme. Juliette Adam, 1895–1908* (Cairo: The Mustafa Kamel School, 1908).

3. Beth Baron summarizes the combination of social and political advantages of such high-level marriages in general, and for this

marriage in particular. "On Mustafa Fahmi's side, the marriage helped . . . solidify the family's local ties and linked their fate to a rising star, one of the Western-educated professionals emerging from the ranks of the provincial notables. Marriages of the Turkish-speaking Ottoman-Egyptian elite to Egyptian professionals was an increasingly common strategy, giving one side financial security and the other higher social status." Beth Baron, *Egypt as a Woman* (Berkeley: University of California Press, 2005), 139.

4. See the first mention of Farid's and Shawish's somewhat enigmatic roles as "inherited symbols' adopted by the Wafd in chapter 1. A unique body of primary source documentation of the controversial relationship between these two individuals themselves during their years in exile can be found in Arthur Goldschmidt, editor and translator, *The Memoirs and Diaries of Muhammad Farid, an Egyptian Nationalist Leader (1868–1919)* (San Francisco: Mellen University Research Press, 1992).

At one point Farid said of Shawish, "This man . . . has no principles and wants to live by whatever means he can. . . . . If he could now return to Egypt and have his livelihood guaranteed, he would not hesitate to go. Indeed, if he could negotiate with the British for a pardon, he would not delay" (p. 422). At a later point, Farid wrote "[It] is not strange that Jawish [*sic*] is trying to take . . . work away from the National Party . . . to put it in the name of a new and different party. In doing so, he aims . . . to have himself elected head of the new group he wants to set up" (pp. 464–465). The most scathing remark came just after World War I: "[T]he man must be watched lest he comment other [more] childish acts," further concluding, "[T]he man is clumsy, stupid, and unsuited to engage in politics at all" (p. 503). Such documented observations make it all the more ironic—indeed enigmatic—that, as early as the first years after World War I, both Farid and Shawish would figure as symbols again and again in the Wafd poster campaign as presumed supporters of Zaghlul's cause. A personal communication from Professor Goldschmidt (July 30, 2015) makes it clear that he too found Shawish's "adoption" in the Wafd posters enigmatic: "He was never friendly to Zaghlul and the Wafd, which he . . . believed would sell out to the British. . . . [Therefore] I am surprised that Jawish [*sic*] would appear on Wafdist posters. . . ."

5. A detailed study of the impact of World War I on Egypt is Malak Badrawi, *Political Violence in Egypt, 1910–1925* (Richmond: Curzon Press, 2000).

6. This chapter's abbreviated account of Zaghlul's political experiences during World War I and into the postwar period is largely based on Janet Terry's seminal publication, *The Wafd: 1919–1952: Cornerstone of Egyptian Political Power* (London: Third World Centre for Research and Publishing, 1982). Other accounts of the early stages of Wafd activity is in Afaf Marsot, *Egypt's Liberal Experiment*, 1977, chapters 2–3, and the more recent book by Ziad Fahmy, *Ordinary Egyptians: Creating the Modern Nation through Popular Culture* (Palo Alto: Stanford University Press, 2011).

7. Terry, *The Wafd*, 46–47.

8. Ibid., 48–49.

9. Ibid., 49.

10. Ibid., 73.

11. 'Abd al-'Aziz Fahmi was the same high official whose name was put forward unsuccessfully with Zaghlul for a possible ministerial post in 1917. 'Ali Shaarawi was a wealthy Egyptian who lent political and material support to the Wafd's early activities. His wife, Huda Shaarawi, gained wide recognition for her role in founding, under the auspices of the Wafd, Egypt's first feminist organization. Despite her prominent position alongside Safiya Zaghlul ín laying down the lines of the Wafd's program for Egyptian women, Huda Shaarawi was not pictured (unlike Zaghlul's wife) in the preelection campaign posters. Caricaturists seized upon her personage, however, when she had a falling out with the Wafd leader (see figure 7.5).

12. Terry, *The Wafd*, 82. An original poster (figure 6.22) from the JWM/Utah collection showing all fourteen members of the Wafd's proposed delegation is discussed in chapter 6.

13. The Wafd's twenty-six-article program is outlined in Terry, *The Wafd*, 87.

14. An obviously separate Watanist communication bearing the signature of Mustafa Kamil's successor in exile, Muhammad Farid, was published as *Mémoires Présentés par le Parti National Égyptien à la Conférence de la Paix à Paris* (Geneva: Édouard Pfeffer, 1919).

15. 'Adli Yakin (variously written as Yegen, 1864–1933) would play a key role as prime minister in the critical period between 1921 and 1922. By that time, the British government would be pushing for a compromise arrangement "behind Zaghlul's back" or, alternatively, through stronger

tactics, including Zaghlul's physical exile when pro-Wafd demonstrations turned violent.

16. Terry, *The Wafd*, 94, quoting a Foreign Office minute interpreting High Commissioner Wingate's dispatch of January 30, 1919 (FO371/3711).

17. See Beth Baron, *Egypt as a Woman*, chapter 5, "The Ladies' Demonstrations," and the LL/Cairo lithograph, figure 2.2.

18. Terry, *The Wafd*, 105–106. A section entitled "Pamphlets, Pamphleteering, and the 'Illicit' Press" in Ziad Fahmy, *Ordinary Egyptians*, 151–153, provides some detail concerning the Wafd's bid to bring "a variety of information serving different short-term and long-term nationalist goals [to public attention]." Fahmy focuses, however, on tumultuous events in the first half of 1919. He makes no mention of the graphic material appearing in Terry's earlier account.

19. Because of the chronological conjuncture here—the first possible reference to the "Wafd Committee of Fourteen" poster in the Marriott Library collection—I have selected at random a lithograph that *may* have been typical of the earliest pro-Zaghlul graphics mentioned here by Terry. This portrait was printed in the *Cairo Punch*, which would play a very significant role in the poster campaign that followed over the next few years. Both the original "Committee of Fourteen" poster and a variety of additional Zaghlul portraits are discussed in chapter 6.

20. See Beth Baron, *Egypt as a Woman*, 123–134. Figures 2.2 and 2.3 are from the LL/Cairo collection.

21. Artistic style in this case, as well as the lithographer's signature, Ahmad Zaʿzûʿ (a principal founder of a group called the "Association for Nationalist Images," which will be discussed) tends to suggest that figure 2.3 is an early harbinger of the coming awareness of a need to shift support away from Zaghlul's political rivals in the Watan Party. When that political move occurred, the artistic style that Zaʿzûʿ used in figure 2.3 will be seen to have moved at the same time.

22. Terry, *The Wafd*, 117 (italics added). Milner, more famous perhaps for his major role in South African affairs, had served previously as an adviser in the Occupation administration in the 1890s.

23. Ibid., 122.

24. Each stage of exchanges between members of the British government as well as between British negotiators and different Egyptian spokesmen vying for influence in the negotiations that eventually led to the end of the protectorate can

be seen in sequence in Terry's chapter 6, pp. 125–152. A 1997 American University in Cairo master's thesis provides a good review of the sometimes bitter interpersonal local political rivalries that Terry outlines. See the digital version of Tonia Rifaey, "An Illustration of the Transitional Period in Egypt during 1919–1924: Political Cartoons in Egypt's Revolutionary History," http://dar.aucegypt.edu/handle/10526/5014. Three striking caricatures noted in Rifaey's thesis, especially figures 7.1 and 7.2, point to emerging rivalries within Wafd leadership ranks. These caricatures, however, date from about two years after the events being described here.

25. Terry, *The Wafd*, 140–141.

26. Ibid., 144, quoting Allenby to Curzon, February 2, 1922 (FO371/7731).

27. Ibid., 146.

28. Probably the fullest discussion of ʿAbd al-Hamid Zaki's career as a publicist/caricaturist *before* the onset of World War I (but *not* the next period of his career that involved him in the Wafd's illustrated campaign propaganda) is in Marilyn Booth's article cited above, "What Is in a Name?" My own treatment of the "disconnect" between his earlier work and his contribution to the Wafd's campaign appears in several sections of the following chapters. A second, clearly more famous name, is that of James Sanua. Sanua's contributions will also be reviewed but, as the discussion unfolds, reasons for my extensive focus on Zaki in several chapters will become apparent.

Chapter 3

1. See note 3 in the Preface describing use of the term "folk imagery" here and elsewhere in the text.

2. Details concerning Zaki and the *Cairo Punch* press between 1907 and 1908 (only the initial stage of a long publishing career) appear in chapter 4. His later contributions linking him to the Wafd campaign posters form an essential part of the "Real Precedents . . ." theme developed in chapter 5.

3. The most basic process of lithographic printing involves drawing images on a flat stone plate using an implement doused with oil, fat, or wax. Limestone was the most commonly used material. The entire stone was then coated with a mixture of acid and gum arabic. Areas not protected by the grease-based image were essentially etched away by chemical action. Applying water to the total surface moistened

the "etched" areas only. When an oil-based ink was rolled on, it would be repelled by the water, adhering only to oily lines and surface of the original drawing. Printing by a mechanical press process then followed.

4. *Honoré Daumier, 1808–1879* (Los Angeles: Armand Hammer Daumier Collection, 1982), 38–46.

5. In *Vive les wagons de troisième classe* (*Long-live the Third-Class Cars*), for example, Monsieur Prud'homme takes more than his space between bedraggled and obviously less privileged train passengers and quips, "On peut y être asphyxié mais jamais assassiné" ("One might be asphyxiated here, but never assassinated"). Ibid., 164–165, from *Le charivari*, March 24, 1865.

6. See in particular the articles in Hans Harder and Barbara Mittler, editors, *Asian Punches: A Transcultural Affair* (New York: Springer, 2013).

7. A recent monograph on the subject is Elizabeth E. Guffey, *Posters: A Global History* (London: Reaktion Books, 2015).

8. A selected example of this would be the Dutch artist Louis Raemaeker's drawings in J. Murray Allison, *Raemaeker's Cartoon History of the War* (London: John Lane, 1919).

9. See, for example, totally contrasting uses of symbolism in two near-contemporary posters, one by a famous Mexican artist (involving both symbolism and some folk imagery) and another (completely abstract symbolism) by a revolutionary Bolshevik artist reproduced in Guffy, *Posters*, 9, 76, respectively.

10. Among the multitude of publications dealing with the extremely popular subject of the Épinal press, most in French, one should mention the less specialized surveys by Armand Lanoux, *Les images d'Épinal* (Paris: B. Grasset, 1969); Henri George, *La belle histoire des images d'Épinal* (Paris: Le Cherche Midi, 1996); and Dennis Martin and Bernard Huin, *Images d'Épinal* (Quebec: Musée de Québec, 1995). The city of Épinal itself maintains an extensive museum devoted to images printed by the Épinal Press.

11. Strong propagandistic undercurrents are obvious in titles of some *Images* artists' drawings during World War I: *Le Beau Régiment*, by A. Bognard in 1915; or *Les Alliés en Campagne*, by H. Carrey, 1914–1916. A recent monograph focuses on specific wartime graphics: Myriam Blanc, *Verdun et la grande guerre par les images d'Épinal* (Paris: Chêne, 2016).

12. René Perrout, *Les images d'Épinal* (Nancy: La Revue Lorraine illustrée, 1912), 49–72.

13. https://fr.wikipedia.org/wiki/Image_d %27Épinal. Although the *Images d'Épinal* tradition is best known for its wide range of drawings reflecting historical and contemporary subjects familiar to French children and adults alike, it was initially launched to print original and attractive playing cards. By the time its fame had spread to the entire population, its production touched such diverse spheres as representations of all artisanal trades with matching letters of the alphabet, cut-out brochures to familiarize and amuse children with specialized social roles, and stereotypic school masters and classrooms. Just as frequently, however, light-hearted scenes used "common-sense" issues to make people laugh at themselves. An early example of the latter would be *Grande Querelle entre la mari et l'épouse: à qui portera la culotte et commandera dans le mènage* (*The Major Quarrel between the Husband and Wife as to Who Will Wear the Pants and Command in the Household*), appearing in October 1820. See Dennis Martin and Bernard Huin, *Images d'Épinal*, 122.

14. See chapter 5, figure 5.10. The Noah's Ark lithograph reproduced here, which bears the name of Muhammad ʿAli al-Jundi as the artist, is from JWM/Utah. An original duplicate of the same poster is in the LL/Cairo collection.

15. Studies of *Punch* are clearly too numerous to list here. A recent work, Patrick Leary, *The Punch Brotherhood: Table Talk and Print Culture in Mid-Victorian London* (London: British Library, 2010), can be compared to an earlier general history by Marion H. Spielman, *The History of Punch* (Detroit: Gale Research, 1969).

16. An *Evening with Punch* (London: Bradbury, Agnew and Oc., 1900).

17. Ibid., 171, February 23, 1889.

18. Ibid., 103, August 3, 1889.

19. Ibid., 165, December 11, 1875. See discussion of same in chapter 1.

20. Elif Elmas, "Teodor Kassab's Adaptation of the Ottoman Shadow Theatre Karagöz," in Harder and Mittler, *Asian Punches*, 245–270. Kassab, born a Greek Ottoman subject, experienced a varied and cosmopolitan career. His biography appears in Elmas's note 18, 247–248. Elmas reported (from another source), "Between 1870 and 1877, nearly 20 satirical journals appeared in the Ottoman Empire. Most . . . were short-lived and ceased after the first issue" (246).

21. Ibid., 255–256.

22. Ibid., 256.

23. Jonathan Guyer, who has written widely on many historical aspects of caricature art in the

Ottoman Empire, suggests that it was Kassab's involvement in political issues, not just the columns of *Hayal,* that ran him afoul of Ottoman authorities and put an end to his publishing activities. Guyer's statement in his January 2017 article in *Le Monde Diplomatique,* "On the Arab Page," raises some questions regarding "transferred influences" from European models in *Hayal.* He wrote, "Ottoman publications, influenced by French and British caricatures, took off in Istanbul and travelled across the ... empire.... Ottoman works, among them *Hayal* ..., were strikingly similar to [drawings from Europe] ... such as those by James Gillray and André Gill."

24. Stanford University's Hoover Institution collection of World War I posters from nine different countries can be accessed at http://infolab .stanford.edu/~mmorten/propaganda/wwi/. However, this extensive collection does not appear to include any material depicting Ottoman forces in the war.

25. Charles Larcom Graves, *Mr. Punch's History of the Great War* (New York: Frederick A. Stokes, 1919).

26. Ibid., 28–29.

27. Ibid., 141.

28. Although the continuing patterns in *Punch's* seemingly endless stream of satirical caricatures aimed at all continents after World War I, including the post–Ottoman Middle East, will not be discussed here, interesting examples of *Punch's* graphic approach to post-1918 Anglo-Egyptian negotiations over the status of the "Four Reserved Points" (one being maintenance of the Anglo-Egyptian condominium in the Sudan) are reproduced in Afaf Marsot's *Egypt's Liberal Experiment,* 77–79.

29. Roy Douglas, *The Great War 1914–1918: The Cartoonists' Vision* (New York: Routledge, 1995), 15.

30. These Balkan conflicts have, of course, their own histories. Briefly, the sultanate had to respond to territorial expansion threats from the Balkan League, which included Greece and the more recently independent former Ottoman provinces of Bulgaria, Serbia, and Montenegro. The debilitating Turkish experience, especially in the First Balkan War, undoubtedly played a role in the subsequent Ottoman alliance with the Germany and Austria in World War I.

31. I am indebted to Professor Recep Boztemür of the Middle East Technical University, Ankara, for providing the reproduction in figure 3.8.

32. Palmira Brummett, "New Woman and Old Hag: Images of Women in the Ottoman Cartoon Space," in Charles Issawi and Bernard

Lewis, editors, *Middle Eastern Political Cartoons* (Princeton: Markus Wiener, 1997), 13–57. The title of Brummett's separate monograph, *Image and Imperialism in the Ottoman Revolutionary Press, 1908–1911* (Albany: SUNY Press, 2000), helps explain her emphasis on contacts between Ottoman culture and the problem of European dominance reflected in this example, as well as most others in her book. Her terms "New Woman" and "Old Hag" here refer mainly to quite different images she finds in caricatures appearing later than the one mentioned here. In the later images she provides, Turkish artists tend to contrast the "new" westernized Turkish woman with negative symbols of the past.

33. "Sultans of Yesterday and Today," http://www .funtrivia.com/playquiz/quiz350400281cf08 .html.

34. Library of Congress Prints and Photographs, Lot 8196.

35. Ibid.

36. See, among other studies covering this important late stage in Ottoman history, Kemal H. Karpat, *The Politicization of Islam: Reconstructing Identity, State, Faith, and Community in the Late Ottoman State* (New York: Oxford University Press, 2001).

37. The British Museum poster collection is catalogued as Acquisition 1948,1214,0.*x*, with a sequence of individual graphics numbered from 1 to the last graphic in the acquisition. All subsequent references to examples I have drawn from the collection will be identified by the abbreviated entry BM 1948,1214,0.*x*, with the corresponding number of the particular graphic. The different types of propaganda posters in the collection can be seen by the different titles, some appearing on the prints, others added by the Museum's cataloguers. *Constitutional Troops Entering Constantinople to Protect Liberty* (BM 1948,1214,0.13) is from an earlier date (probably 1908) by comparison with *Mustafa Kemal Surrounding the Fortifications of the Dardanelles* (BM 1948,1214,0.3), clearly from the World War I period.

38. BM 1948,1214,0.8.

39. Library of Congress, Prints and Photographs Division, Lot 8196. This Library of Congress listing contains eight prints. Of these, only two are unique to the LOC collection, the other six appear to be duplicates of posters in the British Museum's 1948 1214.0. listing.

40. BM 1948,1214,0.10.

41. Marilyn Booth, in her 2013 article, "What's in a Name?" (287–288), poses a very similar

question. She hints at possible earlier influences on Zaki, stemming from his presumed study experiences in Europe and perhaps even close artistic collaboration with other (Italian?) artists. In correspondence with the author, Professor Booth indicates that she was unaware at the time that the post-1908 output of the *Cairo Punch* press produced anything like the quite elementary artwork in the Wafd posters. Thus, this seems to be a starting point for asking the question I pose in stages: what may explain the "disconnect" between the *Cairo Punch* caricatures before and after 1908?

Chapter 4

1. Afaf Marsot's 1971 article, "The Cartoon in Egypt," has been citied in earlier sections of this book. A selection of articles on the subject (for different Middle Eastern countries, including Egypt) was published by Charles Issawi and Bernard Lewis: *Cultural Representations in the Middle East: Political Cartoons* (Princeton, NJ: Markus Wiener, 1997).

2. Figure 4.1 courtesy of the LL/Cairo collection.

3. This supposition stems from the typically Egyptian (Mamluk period) minarets in the background, which bear little resemblance to those in the Turkish capital. Obvious differences between the two architectural styles are described in Annemarie Schimmel, *Islam: An Introduction* (Albany: SUNY Press, 1992), 42–43.

4. Marilyn Booth, "What's in a Name," 277, note 12. Marsot's language (p. 11 of the 1971 article) was even more pointed when she concluded her discussion of the well-known (and markedly eccentric) caricaturist James Sanua: "For a long time after Sanua went into exile [in 1879], the graphic political cartoon disappeared from the Egyptian scene. . . ." Booth countered this claim, stating, "[T]hose who have studied Egyptian satire and the political cartoon in Egypt have neglected . . . *The Cairo Punch* [founded in 1907]."

5. Marsot, Op. cit., 2.

6. Bibliography dealing with Sanua is extensive and very diverse. Worldwide, many libraries hold valuable but incomplete examples of his prolific work. Various published sources include Paul de Baignières's rare book with forty-eight pages of Sanua's original artwork, *L'Egypt satirique: album d'Abu Naddara* (Paris: Imprimerie Lefebvre, 1886), and *La France et son histoire, Paris et ses expositions, par J. Sanua Abou Naddara* (Paris: G. Lefebvre, 1899). Both

obviously antiquarian publications should be compared with Eliane Ettmüller's book, *The Construct of Egypt's National Self in James Sanua's Early Satire and Caricature* (Berlin: Klaus Schwarz, 2012). An example of a very recent article, with illustrations, dealing with Sanua's work is Anna Della Subin and Hussein Omar, "The Egyptian Satirist Who Inspired a Revolution," *New Yorker* (June 6, 2016).

Eliane Ettmüller's article in Harder's and Mittler's *Asian Punches: A Transcultural Affair*, entitled "Abû Nazzâra's Journey from Victorious Egypt to Splendorous Paris: The Making of an Arabic *Punch*," provided most of the background material used here to sketch the broad lines of Sanua's career.

7. Palmira Brummett, *Image and Imperialism in the Ottoman Revolutionary Press, 1908–1911* (Albany: SUNY Press, 2000). Brummett's examples of biting political satire from major gazettes published in Istanbul in this period are far too numerous to discuss here. A quote from her excellent concluding chapter underlines one of the key themes running throughout her book. "Some of the options . . . in the satirical press were conquest and the surrender to European culture, tenacious adherence to the imperfect yet familiar old order, or some form of compromise position along with its concomitant anxiety and cultural schizophrenia" (328). Despite the variety of Ottoman publications from which Brummett drew her examples of satirical caricatures in chapters as wide ranging as "The Comic Sovereign: The Satirical Critique of Authority," and "The Comic Aggressor: The Critique of European Political and Economic Hegemony," almost all suggest very close adherence to European caricatural styles of the period. Although selection here of an example from each of these two foci does little justice to the depth of Brummett's analysis, it does suggest why her title "Image and Imperialism . . ." would be reflected again and again in the pre-1914 Young Turk "revolutionary press." Figure 5.2, p. 120, *At the Museum: Dinosaurs of the Past*, shows Reza Tevfik Bey (a noted writer and intellectual of the period, dressed in fully Western "sporty" garb) lecturing to young, clean-shaven effendis in front of two showcases, one displaying dinosaur skeletons and the other with uniformed traditional autocrats from the Ottoman past. Another example, *Critique of European Political . . . Hegemony (The English Occupation of Egypt in Kalem of 30 September 1909)*, depicts a giant, pipe-smoking, nonchalant British soldier

reclining with booted feet propped on the Pyramids while diminutive, traditionally robed figures decry his lack of respect for obvious symbols of Egypt's past glory (155, figure 6.1).

8. The source used here to review *Awadh Punch* is Mushirul Hasan, *Wit and Humour in Colonial North India* (New Delhi: Nyogi Books, 2007). More recent attention to Indian caricature art in the same period can be found in Part One of Ritu Gairola Khanduri, *Caricaturing Culture in India* (Cambridge: Cambridge University Press, 2014).

9. Hans Harder and Barbara Mittler, *Asian Punches: A Transcultural Affair* (New York: Springer, 2013).

10. Mushirul Hasan, *Wit and Humour*, 35.

11. *Fun* was a Victorian weekly magazine, first published in September 1861. The magazine was founded by the actor and playwright H. J. Byron. It was generally considered competitive with *Punch*.

12. Those familiar with Indian popular culture as it evolved during the first half of the twentieth century will have seen many reiterations of the Mother India image as a symbol of India's desire to obtain respect for its traditional values along with political independence. One of the most famous, from the collection of the Rabindra Bharati Society in Kolkata, India, was Abanindranath Tagore's 1905 watercolor *Bharat Mata* (*Mother India*) reproduced by Mrinalini Sinha on page 3 of her monograph *Specters of Mother India*. Following well-established Indian symbolism, Tagore's traditionally clad Indian woman has four arms, each holding what Sinha called "objects of nationalist aspiration: food, clothing, secular learning, and spiritual knowledge."

These symbolic objects, combined with the simplicity of the image of Mother India, fit the general definition of folk imagery quite well, and can be compared, even with obvious cultural differences, with examples of "Mother Egypt" appearing in later chapters.

13. Ibid., 79.

14. Brummett, *Image and Imperialism*. See discussion of Brummett's selection of satirical graphics, especially those in her chapter "Critique of European Political . . . Hegemony," in note 7 above.

15. Ibid., 132.

16. Afaf Marsot, "The Cartoon in Egypt," 12 (italics added).

17. The most comprehensive recent study is Eliane Ettmüller, *The Construct of Egypt's National Self in James Sanua's Early Satire and Caricature*

(Berlin: Klaus Schwarz, 2012). Pioneering work (in English) on Sanua's career was done by Irene Gendzier, *The Practical Visions of Ya'qub Sanu* (Cambridge, MA: Harvard University Press, 1966).

18. Eliane Ettmüller, "Abû Nazzâra's Journey," 226.

19. Ibid., 219–244.

20. Although Irene Gendzier's study of Sanua's career (*The Practical Visions*, 1966) reflects a quite different set of research concerns from those seen in Eliane Ettmüller's work, many sections of Gendzier's text confirm Sanua's "cosmopolitan" orientation. She notes, for example (69), that Sanua used both French and English in many of his publications and that his *al-'Alam al-islâmiyya*, with the joint title *L'Univers Musulman*, "was published, ironically, entirely in French." Also of note is the fact that *L'Univers Musulman* was published by the Épinal Press in France. Such observations fit with Gendzier's suggestion (69) that "the journals published under his name aspired to capture nothing less than a European audience. . . ."

21. A vital source of primary source documentation covering this initial period and further years of Sanua's art work and writing comes from the work of Prof. Dr. Hans Harder's Heidelberg University team, Project B1, "Gauging Cultural Asymmetries: Asian Satire and the Search for Identity in the Era of Colonialism and Imperialism." As part of her research published in book form in 2012, Eliane Ettmüller worked to obtain permission from Mrs. Eva Milhaud and Prof. Dr. Nagwa Anous to digitize almost the entire corpus of Sanua's journalistic publications through 1910. The collection can be accessed online: https://heidata.uni-heidelberg .de/dataset.xhtml?persistentId=doi:10.11588 /data/10076.

22. Ettmüller, "Abû Nazzâra's Journey," 228–229.

23. Ibid., 230. This drawing appeared in the November 21, 1878, issue.

24. https://heidata.uni-heidelberg.de/dataset .xhtml?persistentId=doi:10.11588/data/10076. This drawing should be compared with a very similar one from March 1879 appearing in Ettmüller, *The Construct of Egypt's National Self*, 2012, 111.

25. The current state of research, including work by Marilyn Booth on Zaki's initial years, suggests that, although the *Cairo Punch* is commonly referenced as being active between 1907 and some point in the 1930s, no library or private collection has preserved actual numbered issues from the long span of time between about 1909

and the end of its publication. Professor Booth's view of the "continuity" problem after 1908 appears in the following note.

26. My own overview here of the *Cairo Punch*'s first year of publication (1907–1908), which is only meant to set the stage for eventual understanding of political caricature and folk imagery in the 1919–1923 Wafd election campaign, reflects my clear dependence on Marilyn Booth's original research published in 2013. The idea that Zaki's "interim" years between 1908 and the reappearance of his work on Egyptian subjects just before and after World War I can help explain the provenance of the Wafd campaign posters may also help clarify the "mystery" of standard references to the dates of *Cairo Punch* publications from 1907 to some point in the early 1930s. Marilyn Booth's email correspondence with the author in the first months of 2016 registers her disappointment when she tried to uncover examples of *Cairo Punch* publications dating later than the 1907–1908 period. In early 2016, she wrote: "It is really frustrating not to have more of the *CP*. I have never seen any reference to it existing beyond the two to three years listed in the *Dar ul-Kutub* catalogue, and they don't have any of the issues listed!" Her later correspondence in January 2016, after seeing examples of Zaki's *post*-1908 work that appear in this book suggested the following: "Your material makes the question of who drew the earlier caricatures even more puzzling to me.... The later [drawings] do seem artistically cruder as well as less politically complicated."

27. Booth, "What's in a Name," 283. Booth also included (291), without specifics, a reference in the well-known contemporary newspaper *al-Mu'ayyad* to the "stellar proprietor ... [Zaki], a former officer in the Egyptian army." In her note 12 (277), Booth cites mention of *al-Siyâsa al-muṣawwara/Cairo Punch* in Philippe de Tarrazi's classic four-volume work, *Tarîkh al-ṣiḥâfa al-'arabiyya* (Beirut: Maṭba'a al-Adabiyya, 1913–1914). Tarrazi's typically ebullient prose compliments the illustrated journal's "splendor and renown," declaring, "Its drawings were beautifully printed and vied with its peers in Europe," [quoted here from Booth's translated extract on pp. 278–279]. This source apparently did not, however, provide information on Zaki's biographical background. Corresponding with Zaki's direct descendants in February, 2019, confirmed the fact that he attended a military school in Egypt and served in the Egyptian army. See paragraph 2 of the Preface.

28. Booth's use of these terms on p. 283 of her article apparently stems from "testimonies" in the *Cairo Punch*'s second issue in 1907. Allusions to prior educational background are based on Zaki's own claims that he had studied drawing in Europe, perhaps in Italy. Booth's quote from the *Cairo Punch* December 15, 1907, issue (282) is particularly intriguing. He wrote, "I travelled [to Europe] to draw upon and drink the water from its source. I came back with fertile seed, well sown in what my hand could do with this art, and what my mind might absorb."

Booth's references to similarities between the *Cairo Punch* drawings and those she observed in the Italian caricatured journal *Il Papagallo* don't necessarily suggest an earlier Italian study experience (and, even more important, *Il Papagallo*'s influence, and possibly even participation in preparing the *Cairo Punch*'s *early* drawings). The fact that Zaki would move his press to Bologna after one year of publication in Cairo does, of course, beg the question of prior contacts in Italy. Marilyn Booth's published paragraphs on the subject (287–288) raise questions along these lines.

29. See the quote from "We and the Foreigners," in the *Cairo Punch*, July 17, 1908 (288–289) and the pithy wording from "al-Inkilîz" ("The English") in the *Cairo Punch*'s first issue. In Booth (290), for example, we find: "The [English] are a people of politicking and duplicity." And, in the same paragraph, "[T]heir duplicity is like wine: weak in the glass, strong in the head."

30. The thirty-seven originals consulted by Professor Booth are held by Stanford University's Hoover Institution. All are from the first period of publication before or shortly after Zaki's press moved to Italy. Booth reported (Op. cit., 274, note 3) that they include nineteen issues dealing with Egypt under British occupation and three reflecting some form of foreign influence in local Egyptian politics. Other caricatured images—all critical of European imperialist tendencies—focus on the Ottoman Empire or the wider international field.

31. Ibid., 296.

32. A second example appearing in Booth's article bears a title equivalent to "Egypt under the Knife," 293–294. It shows John Bull as a surgeon removing infected sores from the (labeled female) body of Egypt on an operating table. Booth translated the Arabic captions describing Egypt's sores as: "The Sudan," "Foreign Companies in Egypt," "The National Debt," "Privileges

Given to Foreigners," and "The People's Ignorance."

33. Ibid., 299.

34. Ibid., 299.

35. Mushirul Hasan, *Wit and Humour*, 77.

36. Booth provides an account of Zaki's ebullient reaction to mention of *Cairo Punch* in the *Review of Reviews*, including his claim to be "accomplishing the duty required of us toward the nation and its noble children . . ." In fact, Booth describes content in the *Review of Reviews* as a regular, almost mechanical "mapping of the world of caricature" (Booth, "What's in a Name," 284–285). Far from lauding Zaki's political audacity, reproduction of his caricatures there appeared under the somewhat condescending title, *A Curious Egyptian View of International Politics.*

37. United States Library of Congress, Prints and Photographs Division, Lot 8196.

38. Booth discusses *Modern Civilization* on p. 288 of her article. Although she gives an exact publication date (July 9, 1908), it appears to have been included in a "special issue" that she was unable to find among the Hoover Institution collection of the *Cairo Punch*'s earliest issues.

39. Booth, "What's in a Name," 288–289 from *Naḥnu wa'l-ajânib*, July 17, 1908.

40. Ibid., 292.

41. On March 4, 2016, Booth wrote to the author: "What I suspect is that Zaki started out with this journalistic/political ambition and agenda but then ended up just needing to make money, or getting fed up with the political side, or something we don't know. It seems, from the material you've found, that it just ends up more or less as a business, though maybe retaining at least a whiff of anti-colonial fervor."

Chapter 5

1. See the original citation of these British Museum holdings, chapter 3, note 37.

2. See discussion of Brummett's monograph, chapter 4, note 7.

3. British Museum (1948 1214,0.15) *Arafat Day*. The *maḥmil* is a palanquin or camel-borne litter. Provision of a *maḥmil*, richly decorated, is an honor traditionally assumed by the rulers of Egypt and Syria in association with their responsibility to oversee protection of pilgrims traveling from their provinces to perform the hajj.

4. A second *maḥmil* scene by Cairo lithographer Ahmad Za'zû' tends to strengthen this

suggestion (LL/Cairo collection, not reproduced here). Although there is a certain degree of splendor in Za'zû''s representation of the four-camel procession on the way to Mecca, accompanying onlookers (effendis and "country folk" mixed, almost all males, two women only in the foreground, three veiled women in the distance) show scarcely any enthusiasm as they either chat or watch the passing column.

5. BM 1948,1214.0.11.

6. This question is not just rhetorical. Beginning sometime after 1908, the *Cairo Punch*'s publication of propaganda posters supporting the Ottoman imperial cause (particularly visible in military moves during the Balkan Wars) is a matter of documented fact (see chapter 3, figures 3.10 and 3.11).

7. BM 1948,1214,0.25. All individuals whose photographic facial features were "inserted" into the lithograph, including the Egyptian Commander of the Pilgrimage, bore titles. These were: Nur al-Din Bey, a town administrator (*mukhtâr*), and three doctors, one bearing the surname Zaki, possibly the artist's father.

8. Library of Congress Posters and Photographs. Lot 8096, *Muhammad V and HH Khedive of Egypt Review the Ottoman Fleet* (not reproduced here).

9. Ibid., *H. H. Hadji Abbas Helmi II, Khedive of Egypt at Madina.*

10. This railway was constructed during Abdul Hamid II's reign using donations from Muslims from all over the world. Its primary, publicly proclaimed purpose was to help transport pilgrims from Syria to Medina. Its strategic importance, of course, forms part of the history of Ottoman participation in World War I.

11. BM 1948,2014,0.7.

12. A popular definition of "keepsake" should suffice to justify use of this term to describe the otherwise uncategorized original artwork reproduced here. A "keepsake," according to *Merriam Webster*, is "something [kept] to help . . . remember a person, place, or event." This simple wording should be compared with Professor Booth's citation of a notice that appeared "in many . . . issues" of the *Cairo Punch* from 1908 forward: "If you wish to adorn . . . your home or make for yourself a memento to last a lifetime, simply send a photograph [for the *Cairo Punch* to] . . . make a perfect [competitively priced] image. Booth, op. cit., 292.

13. The fact that posters with the identifying mark Sharika al-Ṣurûr al-Waṭaniyya list the names of several local printers together leads me to take

the term *sharika* here literally. Several printers must have formed a partnership with Ahmad Zaʿzūʿ, perhaps contributing funds and labor to produce prints sold (for some form of profit) under the joint auspices of the small-scale commercial group. Al-Jundi's representation of Noah's Ark here is the same lithograph that, because of its obvious reflections of folk imagery, appeared as figure 3.3 in chapter 3.

14. The Night Journey, including the first stage when al-Burâq bore the Prophet from Mecca to Jerusalem and thence to heaven, is the subject of the *Surat al-Isrâ'* in the Qur'an. Accounts of the *miʿrâj* appear in numerous references in the *ḥadîth* literature, legally accepted reports of the deeds and sayings of Muhammad. There is a surviving example of *Cairo Punch* publisher ʿAbd al-Hamid Zaki's version of the *miʿrâj* preserved in the LL/Cairo collection. Zaki used symbols and artistic styles that are quite similar to those in figure 5.11.

15. A different version of this well-known epic emphasizing the victory of good over evil (often involving ʿAntara's devotion to the feminine ideal represented by ʿAbla, whom he valiantly defends with his sword) can be seen in an anonymously published lithograph, not reproduced here, in the LL/Cairo collection.

16. Assignment of a pre-1914 date for this Zaʿzūʿ lithograph involves once again a hypothetical assumption. Zaʿzūʿ's identifying mark here is his name followed by the phrase "and his associates." As we shall see, almost all *post*-1918 lithographs by the same artist bear, after his name, the by then oft-repeated name "[the] Association for National[ist] Illustrations."

17. Figure 5.15 is from the LL/Cairo collection of lithographs.

18. BM 1948,2014,0.4. Although this image was printed without the usual identifying the *Cairo Punch* marginal caption seen in the early Bologna period, ʿAbd al-Hamid Zaki's signature is visible in the lower right-hand corner. The fact that it is undated presents a challenge. Obviously, it postdates Mustafa Kamil's death in 1908, but it bears no resemblance at all to the type of political caricature work Zaki was doing at that time. Focal attention on Kamil's political successor, Muhammad Farid, who was exiled to Istanbul in 1912, is only one factor suggesting that the poster may have been done at that time. Perhaps more persuasive for assigning a date near that time is the artistic style. Because I argue that Zaki was just beginning to shift his artistic style by 1909 in the direction of Ottoman prototypes, his *In Memory*

poster may reflect this new stylistic trend. The poster could, therefore, be part of his evolving working style by the time Farid was welcomed in Istanbul as the continuing standard bearer of Kamil's Watan Party, namely, in or around 1912.

19. Shawish has already been mentioned several times as one of Kamil's presumed (but clearly problematic) successors representing the Watan Party. This controversial figure, with an attempt to explain *why* his symbolic presence was going to continue to be important to the Wafd movement, will appear several times in the review of the JWM/Utah and LL/Cairo posters in chapter 6.

20. These stereotypic slogans include statements such as the (paraphrased) words of Farid Bey on the right: "Dear friends! Raise up your voices [for] the *umma* [so it will be able to] govern itself following what the *baṭal* [lit. "hero," meaning Kamil] established for us as the meaning of the true nationalism."

Chapter 6

1. Marsot, "The Cartoon in Egypt," 2.

2. The two main divisions proposed here are (1) political portraits and symbolism and (2) favored folk imagery. The latter will also consider specific events that marked key developments in the Wafd's election bid, gender images, and diverse social groupings. Finally, there will be several posters showing individual members surrounding Saad Zaghlul at what appear to be different stages of the Wafd campaign from the earliest date in 1919 to the eve of the actual 1923–1924 election.

3. All of these individuals were protagonists featured in Zaki's earlier *In Memory of the Late Moustafa Kamel Pasha*, figure 5.16.

4. The surviving original documents in *Mémoires du parti national Égyptien* attest that Farid would have been more of an opponent than a benevolent supporter of Zaghlul's cause—a role that could only be implied symbolically in this poster. A complementary approach to this essential point is developed in note 5.

5. On Shawish's "renegade" (and certainly *persona non grata*) status in the eyes of Farid, see chapter 2, note 4. The translator of Farid's memoirs, Professor Arthur Goldschmidt, offered personal help on several questions I posed to him in correspondence. He forwarded, for example, a valuable anecdote on Zaghlul's own view of Shawish, appearing in his transcription of a letter to the *Times* that leaves no doubt that

Shawish and Zaghlul never saw eye to eye. Goldschmidt described the January 26, 1929, letter to the *Times* (close to the time of Shawish's death) as follows: "The anonymous correspondent, who lived in Cairo and was probably British, thinks that Shawish was living in Berlin after the war. . . . When his imminent return to Egypt was announced in 1924, Saad Zaghlul ordered that he should be forbidden to land, but he slipped through the cordon and appeared, penniless and decidedly battered, in Cairo. A few weeks later he was appointed Controller of Elementary Education, settled down to work, and soon proved himself . . . an energetic educationist, unsoured by his experiences." This makes it clear that Shawish never played an actual role in the early organization of the Wafd. Moreover, he was very much *persona non grata* in the eyes of both Muhammad Farid and Zaghlul himself. Goldschmidt's added comment also makes one wonder about Shawish's ubiquitous presence in the Wafd posters: "It sounds as though he wasn't exactly a Wafdist."

6. 'Abduh served as Grand Mufti of Egypt between 1899 and 1905 and was the author of several major theological works recognized throughout the Islamic World. Al-Afghani, originally from Iran, had gained as early as the 1870s and 1880s an international reputation for his anticolonial stance and call for Islamic renewal. Although both supported Egypt's nascent bid (between 1879 and 1882) to liberate itself, to my knowledge neither had more than passing acquaintanceship with Zaghlul in the earlier years of his career. On these two important figures, see Philip Mattar, *Encyclopedia of the Modern Middle East and North Africa*, 2nd ed. (Detroit: MacMillan, 2004), vol. 1, 23–24, 51–53.

7. This was a formal administrative office (as opposed to ascribed ascendancy justifying the religious title and functions of mufti) created in 1895 to oversee proper ordering of religious pronouncements (pl.: *fâtâwa*) according to Islamic procedures.

8. 'Ikrîsha was mentioned in chapter 5 in the context of apolitical keepsake lithographs, specifically for his scenes of Samson and Delilah.

9. In 1920, this smaller version of what became a monumental statue in Ramses Square in 1928 (moved eventually to the Nile bridge near Cairo University) won a prize in an international sculpture competition in France where Mukhtar had studied nearly ten years before; Beth Baron, *Egypt as a Woman*, 67–68. The famous sculptor's work is also discussed in Donald Malcolm Reid,

Contesting Antiquity in Egypt (Cairo: American University in Cairo Press, 2015), 46–47.

10. Although this poster essentially only "appropriates" the sculptor's intention to work symbolism into his visions of Egypt's identity, several of Mukhtar's intended themes in his original 1920 statue would gradually filter into Wafd iconography. Mukhtar's depiction of a female figure representing Egypt was not in itself innovative. His choice to eliminate any suggestion of the need for any particular form of veiling here, however, definitely did have symbolic implications. These would be reflected in different ways in a number of other Wafd campaign posters. As for the second symbolic element—Egypt's close association with its Pharaonic heritage—Mukhtar's incorporation of the Sphinx in his 1920 statuary grouping came two years ahead of an event which drew world attention to Egypt's archaeological treasures: Howard Carter's discovery of the tomb of Tutankhamun. When later Wafd posters began reworking "serious" Pharaonic symbols to fit the simple needs of folk imagery (see, for example, figures 6.16 and 6.17), it is possible, as Professor Donald Reid suggested to the author, that attention to what was otherwise a highly limited scholarly field had begun to filter down to popular levels.

11. George Swan, *Lacked Ye Anything?: A Brief Story of the Egypt General Mission* (London: Morgan and Scott, 1913). A later edition, equally "apolitical," appeared as *In Troublous Times: Sequel to Lacked Ye Anything?* (London: Egypt General Mission, 1923).

12. This, in contrast to what one sees in several illustrated newspapers active by the mid-1920s and throughout the interwar period. Some of these, with pictorial examples, will be discussed in the concluding chapter.

13. Given the *Cairo Punch's* early (1907–1908) and obvious jibes against the British, this probably reflects post-1918 artists' need to follow a new set of political guidelines, first to avoid further alienation of the British, and second to garner wider support from politically moderate as well as minimally informed popular viewers.

14. Janice Terry, *The Wafd*, 139, 149, mentions two occasions when Zaghlul's main political rival, 'Adli Yakin, was either hosted at the Continental (Zaghlul being "spotted motoring by the Hotel twice" in the fall of 1921, just prior to his second exile) or used the hotel when he (Yakin) joined the movement to found the conservative (Liberal Constitutionalist) party alternative to the Wafd in October, 1922.

15. Baron, *Egypt as a Woman*, 194–195. Whatever Zaghlul's motivation in sending this letter of recognition to the founder of the Society of Egyptian Ladies' Awakening, Baron's account of Labiba Ahmad's role up to the time of his death in 1927 contains multiple references to the way in which her Islamic leanings and those of her society "set [her] apart from the secular nationalists." Thus, the photograph of Labiba with Safia, both clad in very conservative style associated with Islamic modesty, which appeared in *Laṭāʾif al-Muṣawwara* on October 16, makes the image in figure 6.9 all the more enigmatic (Baron, *Egypt as a Woman*, 149).

16. Ibid., 194. Sections of Baron's quoted account are drawn from the October 1922 issue of *al-Nahḍa al-Nisāʾiyya*.

17. The highly venerated fourteenth-century Sultan Hassan Mosque and Madrasa on the left and the nineteenth-century al-Rifaʿi Mosque, finally completed under Khedive ʿAbbas II, on the right.

18. One wonders whether ʿAbd al-Hamid Zaki let his memory wander back to the drawing he did for one of the 1907 issues of (the then totally satirical) *Cairo Punch* in which near-transparent veiling was described as openly flirtatious; cf. chapter 4, note 34.

19. These posters are discussed in the last section of the chapter, "Winnowing before the Elections."

20. See note 10, this chapter, and multiple discussions of "Egypt as a Woman" in Beth Baron, *Egypt as a Woman*.

21. Beth Baron, *Egypt as a Woman*, 61, reproduced, for example, Sanua's 1894 *Illusion Détruite* in which the frightening black-robed, almost haunted, image of Egypt with a body-length veil tries to block the female form of England the occupier with the hoped-for help of idealized images of France and Russia. Sanua's subject in *Illlusion Détruite* had to do with high-level alliances just taking shape in European politics twenty years earlier. Its relevance to popular concerns inside Egypt would have been minimal.

22. Seriously damaged portions of the original margins, plus faded characters identifying the artist make provenance difficult to establish. There appear to be vague traces of Zaʿzūʿ's name.

23. Figures 6.13 and 6.14 are both from the LL/Cairo collection.

24. Use of the term *ʾanāṣir* here should not be taken as a sign of concern for *gender* equality, although the party did establish a women's branch led by prominent women such as Safiya Zaghlul herself and the prominent Wafd member Huda Shaarawi. The precise intention of the artist here

is not completely clear, since *ʿunṣur* commonly refers to racial or ethnic distinctions, and the key term remains "unity," not necessarily "equality."

25. Beyond this poster, two other lithographs in the JWM/Utah collection—not reproduced here—document the Wafd's purposeful association with the World Organization of the Scout Movement (itself newly founded in 1922 by Robert Baden-Powell). These posters both show marching formations of young scouts. Only boy scouts are pictured, although Girl Guides were presumed to be part of the federation that Baden-Powell founded. No specific written captions link the latter posters to the Wafd. The "presence" (as inset portraits) of Prince Tusun in one, and Saad Zaghlul with Prince Muhammad ʿAli in the other, however, imply some form of political message.

26. Janice Terry's coverage of such personal political divisions was reviewed in chapter 2. More information, with some additional names and circumstances of persons represented in this last group of posters, appeared in Tonia Rifaey's 1997 MA thesis, also cited in chapter 2. Many caricatures documenting growing rifts with political opponents of the Wafd, as well as rivalries within the party, appear in the Rifaey's thesis. Several of these are reproduced in the Conclusion.

27. Figure 6.22 is the only Wafd poster in the collection announcing in print that proceeds from its sale (at one piaster each) would be donated to charities for the poor in Giza.

28. On Coptic involvement in the Wafd's early stages, see Phillip Mattar, *Encyclopedia*, vol. 1, 640–641.

29. But two of these staunch loyalists would also leave the party in later years: Muhammad Mahmud and Hamid al-Basil. Mahmud was first, moving from Wafdist leadership near the end of Zaghlul's life to become head of the Liberal Constitutionalist Party. On Mahmud as member of the Wafd, see Phillip Mattar, *Encyclopedia*, vol. 3, 1468–1469. Al-Basil became Wafdist vice president of Egypt's first elected chamber of deputies in 1924 and stayed on as vice president of the Wafd until he too left the party in the early 1930s.

30. Namely, the triangle of three above and to the side of the figure of Zaghlul: Hamid al-Basil, Ismaʿil Sidqi, and Muhammad Mahmud.

31. See chapter 2, note 25.

32. Fathallah Barakat is in the upper left corner.

Conclusion

1. A number of surveys of Egyptian caricaturists' work, most concentrating on the mid- and

especially later decades of the twentieth century, could be cited. Among them are ʿAbdullah al-Nâʾîm *Hikayât fiʾl-fakâhati waʾl-kârîkâtîr* (*Cairo*: Dâr al-ʿUlûm wa Tawzi, 2009) and Charles Vial, *Cairicature* (Cairo: Institut Français d'Archéologie Orientale, 1997).

2. El Hakk's and Alleaume's division of their examples into descriptive categories ("Traffic Jams," "Doctors," "The Demographic Problem, etc.) clearly suggests that the subjects deal with "daily images" in Egypt during the period they were studying—the 1980s.

"Folk imagery," as used in the main chapters of this book, was defined at the outset as an intentional composition of images meant to be understandable, and indeed "comfortable" for a broad, unsophisticated audience. Only the first part of this definition, implying immediately understandable images, would apply to use of the term "daily imagery" here. Perhaps the added component of humor helped make up for the *less-than-comforting* messages conveyed in "daily imagery" drawings increasingly offered by Egyptian caricaturists.

3. Marsot, "The Cartoon in Egypt," 13.

4. Baron, *Egypt as a Woman*, 69–74, 89–93. On page 89, Baron states, *al-Lataif* "covered a range of subjects: crime, charity, sports, ceremonies, and funerals. The story of Egyptian nationalism as narrated by Wafdists provided the overarching frame for photos." A third valuable source for reconstructing the early stages of twentieth-century political caricatures in Egypt would be *al-Fukâha* ("Joking," or "Humor"). A quote from Jonathan Guyer's blog, *Oum Cartoon: Caricature and Comics from Egypt, Mother of the World*, on September 1, 2015, indicates the degree to which even specialists are still discovering sources to build a more complete picture of caricature art in early-twentieth-century Egypt. "We know precious little about *Al Fokaha*," he wrote, adding, "Google hasn't helped ... [and] Arabic histories of political cartoons ... don't even note [its] existence. How have cartoon historians missed this?" By a stroke of good fortune, it would appear, the J. Willard Marriott Library of the University of Utah has in its collection bound volumes of *al-Fukâha* covering (with gaps) the first half of the 1930s.

5. https://www.encyclopedia.com/humanities/encyclopedias-almanacs-transcripts-and-maps/lataif-al-musawwara-magazine.

6. ʿAbdullah al-Nâʾîm (hereafter Abdullah al-Naim) *Hikayât fiʾl-fakâhati waʾl-kârîkâtîr* (Cairo: Dâr al ʿUlûm wa Tawzi, 2009) and Tonia Rifaey, "An Illustration of the Transitional Period in Egypt during 1919–1924: Political Cartoons in Egypt's Revolutionary History," MA thesis, American University in Cairo, 1997. http://dar.aucegypt.edu/handle/10526/5014.

7. To give an example, one finds in Baron, *Egypt as a Woman*, 78–79, a reproduction of a caricature published on June 25, 1923 (just before the elections). It shows a woman who, Baron observes, was most certainly Safiya Zaghlul objecting strenuously to a new law of assembly, perceived by the Wafd as thwarting their ongoing campaign.

8. I am indebted to Ms. Tonia Rifaey for responding to my request for information regarding her research and granting permission to reproduce several *al-Kashkul* caricatures from in her AUC master's thesis.

9. Tonia Rifaey, "An Illustration of the Transitional Period," 139, 240. Translations from the colloquial Egyptian are taken directly from Rifaey's text.

10. Illustration reproduced in Arthur Goldschmidt, et al., editors, *Re-Envisioning Egypt, 1919–1952* (Cairo: American University of Cairo Press, 2005), facing p. 350.

11. *Al-Kashkûl*, December 14, 1923, in Tonia Rifaey, op. cit., 1997, 279.

12. *Al-Lataif*, July 7, 1924.

13. *Al-Lataif*, June 9, 1924. See discussion of the situation pictured here in Baron, *Egypt as a Woman*, 166–174.

14. ʿAbdul Sâmʿi Barîshah, *Abyaḍ wa aswad* (Cairo: Ruz al-Yusuf, 1955). The caption here reads: "Tomorrow the Constitutional Committee will be debating the [possibility of a] republican system." An approximate translation of the colloquial Egyptian section in the caption (based on Tonia Rifaey's suggestion) might be: "He lost his head even before the train reached him and ran him over."

The many descriptions of Masri Effendi indicate the wide diversity in opinions of what he came to (and still does) represent. These range from Afaf Marsot's "Mr. Average Egyptian ... short, slightly rotund ..., [who] symbolized the middle-class citizen as opposed to the rural inhabitant ..." to "the grumpy yet jovial character that embodied Egyptian public opinion ..." mentioned in the Cairo *Community Times* edition of January 9, 2016.

BIBLIOGRAPHY

Egyptian Newspapers, and Library and Private Collection Holdings

The British Museum, London
Al-Fukâha
Al-Kashkûl
Al-Laṭâ'if al-muṣawwara
United States Library of Congress, Washington, D.C.
J. Willard Marriott Library of the University of Utah
  Special Collections, Salt Lake City
Lesley Lababidi, early twentieth-century Egyptian
  lithographs, private collection, Cairo

Books and Articles

'Abd al-Nâ'îm, 'Abdullah. *Hikayât fi'l fukâhati wa'l-
  kârîkâtîr.* Cairo: Dar al-'Ulûm l'il-Nashr wa
  Tawzi, 2009.
Allison, J. Murray. *Raemaeker's Cartoon History of the
  War.* London: John Lane, 1919.
Badawi, Jamal. *Tarîkh al-wafd.* Cairo: Dâr al-Shurûq,
  2003.
Badrawi, Malak. *Isma'il Sidqi, 1875–1950: Pragmatism
  and Vision in Twentieth Century Egypt.* Rich-
  mond, Surrey: Curzon Press, 1996.
———. *Political Violence in Egypt, 1910–1925.* Rich-
  mond, Surrey: Curzon Press, 2000.
Barishah, 'Abdul Sâmi'. *Abyaḍ wa aswad.* Cairo: Ruz
  al-Yusuf, 1955.
Baron, Beth. *Egypt as a Woman: Nationalism, Gender,
  and Politics.* Berkeley: University of California
  Press, 2005.
Blanc, Myriam. *Verdun et la grande guerre par les
  images d'Épinal.* Paris: Chêne, 2016.

Booth, Marilyn. "What's in a Name? Branding
  Punch in Cairo, 1908," in Hans Harder and Bar-
  bara Mittler, editors, 271–303, *Asian Punches:
  A Transcultural Affair.* New York: Springer, 2013.
Brummett, Palmira. *Image and Imperialism in the
  Ottoman Revolutionary Press, 1908–1911.* Albany,
  NY: SUNY Press, 2000.
———. "New Woman and Old Hag: Images of
  Women in the Ottoman Cartoon Space,"
  in Charles Issawi and Bernard Lewis, editors,
  13–57, *Middle Eastern Political Cartoons.* Prince-
  ton: Markus Wiener, 1997.
Cannon, Byron. *The Politics of Law and the Courts
  Nineteenth-Century Egypt.* Salt Lake City: University of Utah Press, 1988.
———. "*Transfert de valeurs des paires aux proches*,"
  in Alain Roussillon, editor, 163–179, *Entre
  réforme sociale et mouvement national.* Cairo:
  CEDEJ, 1995.
de Baignières, Paul. *L'Égypte satirique: Album
  d'Abou Naddara.* London: British Museum
  (limited private printing), 1886.
Deeb, Marius. *Party and Politics in Egypt: The Wafd
  and Its Rivals, 1919–1979.* London: Ithaca Press,
  1979.
Ettmüller, Eliane Ursula. "Abû Nazzâra's Journey
  from Victorious Egypt to Splendorous Paris:
  The Making of an Arabic *Punch*," in Hans
  Harder and Barbara Mittler, editors, 219–244,
  Asian Punches: A Transcultural Affair. New
  York: Springer, 2013.
———. "Caricature and Egypt's Revolution of
  25 January 2011," *Zeithistorische Forschungen/
  Studies in Contemporary History* (September

2012). https://zeithistorische-forschungen.de
/1-2012/id=4469.

———. *The Construct of Egypt's National Self in
James Sanua's Early Satire and Caricature.* Berlin: Klaus Schwarz, 2012.

An Evening with "Punch." London: Agnew, 1900.

Fahmy, Ziad. *Ordinary Egyptians.* Palo Alto, CA:
Stanford University Press, 2011.

El Hakk, Farida Gad, and Ghislaine Alleaume. *Essayons d'en rire.* Cairo: CEDEJ, 1982.

George, Henri. *La belle histoire des images d'Épinal.*
Paris: Le Cherche Midi, 1996.

Goldschmidt, Arthur, editor and translator.
*The Memoirs and Diaries of Muhammad Farid,
an Egyptian Nationalist Leader* (1868–1919). San
Francisco: Mellen University Research Press,
1992.

———. et al., editors. *Re-Envisioning Egypt, 1919–
1952.* Cairo: American University of Cairo
Press, 2005.

Graves, Charles Larcom. *Mr. Punch's History of the
Great War.* New York: Frederick A. Stokes,
1919.

Guffy, Ellizabeth E. *Posters: A Global History.* London: Reaktion Books, 2015.

Harder, Hans, and Barbara Mittler, editors. *Asian
Punches: A Transcultural Affair.* New York:
Springer, 2013.

Honoré Daumier, 1808–1879. Los Angeles: Armand
Hammer Daumier Collection, 1982.

Karpat, Kemal H. *The Politicization of Islam: Reconstructing Identity, State, Faith, and Community
in the Late Ottoman State.* New York: Oxford
University Press, 2001.

Martin, Denis, and Bernard Huin. *Images d'Épinal.*
Québec: Musée de Québec, 1995.

Mattar, Philip, Editor in Chief. *Encyclopedia of
Modern Middle East and North Africa,* 2nd ed.
Detroit: Thomson Gale, 2004.

Hasan, Mushirul. *Wit and Humour in Colonial North
India.* New Delhi: Nyogi Books, 2007.

Issawi, Charles, and Bernard Lewis, editors. *Middle
Eastern Political Cartoons.* Princeton: Markus
Wiener, 1997.

Kamil, Ali. *Egyptian-French Letters Addressed to
Mme. Juliette Adam, 1895–1908.* Cairo: Mustafa
Kamel School, 1908.

Leary, Patrick. *The Punch Brotherhood: Table Talk
and Print Culture in Mid-Victorian London.* London: British Library, 2010.

Marsot, Afaf Lutfi al-Sayyid. "The Cartoon in Egypt."
Comparative Studies in Society and History 13,
no. 1 (January 1971):2–15

———. *Egypt's Liberal Experiment.* Berkeley: University of California Press, 1977

———. *Egypt in the Reign of Muhammad Ali.* New
York: Cambridge University Press, 1984.

*Mémoires présentés par le parti national Égyptien à la
conférence de la paix à Paris.* Geneva: Édouard
Pfeffer, 1919.

*Oudh Punch. A Selection from the Illustrations Which
Have Appeared in the Oudh Punch from 1877 to
1881.* Lucknow: Oudh Punch, 1881.

Pollard, Lisa. *Nurturing the Nation: The Family Politics of Modernizing, Colonizing, and Liberating
Egypt, 1805–1923.* Berkeley: University of California Press, 2005.

Rifaey, Tonia. "An Illustration of the Transitional
Period in Egypt during 1919–1924: Political
Cartoons in Egypt's Revolutionary History"
(Master's thesis, American University in Cairo,
1997) http://dar.aucegypt.edu/handle/10526
/5014.

Ryzova, Lucie. *The Age of the Efendiyya: Passages to
Modernity in National-Colonial Egypt.* Oxford:
Oxford University Press, 2014.

Sinha, Mrinalini. *Specters of Mother India.* Durham,
NC: Duke University Press, 2006.

Swan, George. *Lacked Ye Anything?: A Brief Story of
the Egypt General Mission.* London: Morgan
and Scott, 1913.

———. *In Troublous Times: Sequel to Lacked Ye
Anything?* London: Egypt General Mission,
1923.

Terry, Janice. *The Wafd: 1919–1952.* London:
Third World Centre for Research and
Publishing,1982.

Twyman, Michael. *Breaking the Mould: The First
Hundred Years of Lithography. The Panizzi Lectures, 2000.* London: British Library, 2001.

Vatikiotis, P. J. *The Modern History of Egypt.* Baltimore: Johns Hopkins University Press, 1991.

Vial, Charles. *Cairicature.* Cairo: Institut Français
d'Archéologie Orientale, 1997.

INDEX

Egyptian delegation to Paris peace talks, 10, 14–15, *98*, 99, 116n11; elected prime minister, 10; and Farid, 15; and Fuad I, 13; independence of Egypt, xv, 12; marriage, 11–12, 116n3; and Milner Commission, 18, 19; moderation of, 20; as *ra'īs* (head) of Fatherland, *16*, 18; return after end of protectorate, 20; return to deal with Yakin threat, 19, 81, *81–82*; and Shawish, 124n5; symbolic supporters of, 14; Wafd leaders distancing selves from, 96; during wartime protectorate, 12–13

Zaghlul, Saad in posters: commemorating events, 80–84, *81–82*, *84–85*, 86; in interwar period, 104, *105*, 107–8, *107–9*; "keepsake art," 63; as minister of education, 54; with Mother Egypt, *88*, 89, 90, 91, *91*, 93; in "official," 15, *16*, 19, 74–75, *75–76*, 77, *78–81*, *79–80*, 90–91, *91*, 93; political propaganda, 95, *97*; in popular illustrated press, 104; Wafd movement after 1918, 15, *81*, 81–82, 94–95, *96*, 99, *100*, 117n19

Zaghlul, Safiya: as "*ra'īsa*," *16*, 18; in Wafd posters, 15, *82*, 83–84, *84*, 87, *87*, 127n7; Wafd program for women, 116n11, 126n24; Woman's March (1919), 15

Zaghlul . . . and Mister Swan, 77, *79–80*, *80*
Zaghlul and Portraits of Religious Scholar Supporters, 77, *78*
Zaghlul and (Presumed) Wafdist Supporters with the 1920 Mukhtar Statue, 77, *79*, 125n9

Zaghlul Departing for Malta and Second Exile, 82, *82–83*
Zaghlul "Imposes" his Representation on the Backward Sudan, 107, *107*
Zaki, 'Abd al-Hamid: audience targeted by, 51, 52, *53*; background, 22–23, 51, 122nn27–28; characteristics of career between 1908 and World War I, 42–43; commemoration of becoming *ḥājjī*, 60, *60*; and Denshawai scandal, 8; folk imagery posters, 56–57, *58*, *86–87*, 86–88; importance, xii; and "keepsake art," 62–63, 124n14; on *The Modern Civilization of Europe: France in Morocco and England in Egypt,* 54; Ottoman posters by, 35, *36–38*, 38; posters unconnected to Egyptian subjects, 51; prewar posters with political content, 70–72, *71*, 124n18; reviews in *Review of Reviews* and *New York Times*, 53, 123n36; support for Wafd, 54, *54–55*, 69–72, *71*, 92, *94*, 95

Za'zū', Ahmad: *Abraham's Sacrifice (II),* 63, *64*, 124n13; assigning date to works of, 124n16; *Broad Representation of Egyptian Women with Mixed-Gender Musical Group,* 92, *94–95*, *96*; *Egypt Rescued from Assailants on the Nile,* 69, *70*; founder of Association for Nationalist Images, 117n21; *maḥmil* image, 123n4; *Noah's Ark (I),* 63, *65*, *66*; *Zaghlul . . . and Mister Swan,* 77, *79–80*, *80*

Ziwar, Ahmed Pasha, 13